STANDING
GROUND

ALSO BY JOHN LEAX:

The Task of Adam *(poetry)*
In Season and Out *(journal)*
Nightwatch *(fiction)*
Country Labors *(poetry)*

STANDING GROUND

A Personal Story of Faith and Environmentalism

JOHN LEAX

ZondervanPublishingHouse

Grand Rapids, Michigan

A Division of HarperCollins*Publishers*

STANDING GROUND
Copyright © 1991 by John Leax

Requests for information should be addressed to:
Zondervan Publishing House
1415 Lake Drive S.E.
Grand Rapids, Michigan 49506

Library of Congress Cataloging-in-Publication Data

Leax, John.
  Standing ground : a personal story of faith and environmentalism /
John Leax.
    p. cm.
  ISBN 0-310-53791-6 (paper)
  1. Leax, John. 2. Environmentalists—Genesee River Valley (Pa. and
N.Y.)—Biography. 3. Human ecology—Genesee River Valley (Pa.
and N.Y.)—Moral and ethical aspects. 4. Human ecology—
Genesee River Valley (Pa. and N.Y.)—Religious aspects—
Christianity. 5. Radioactive waste disposal—Genesee River Valley
(Pa. and N.Y.) 6. Christian biography—Genesee River Valley (Pa.
and N.Y.) I. Title.
    GF16.L43A3+1991
    363.7'0092—dc20
    [B]   91–17165
                                                                      CIP

Cover designed by Foster Design Associates

 **Printed on Recycled Paper**

Printed in the United States of America

91 92 93 94 95 / ML / 8 7 6 5 4 3 2 1

for Melissa

Be thou exalted, O God,
above the heavens:
let thy glory be
above all the earth
Psalm 57:11

Prologue
The Light That Harms
May 1991

I own four and one-half acres of woods on a hillside west of the Genesee River in the town of Caneadea. I call them Remnant Acres because I intend them to be standing when all other area woods are lost to development. I know this intention is symbolic; I haven't the power to preserve the woods from encroachment, but it is also practical and real, for a symbolic action can be seen and understood. I have committed myself to this intention because I believe the earth is the Lord's and that I am responsible for preserving and caring for the small portion of it I have been given to husband.

My woods aren't pristine. Years ago they were logged. Like other woods around here, they date from no further back than the turn of the century. I have built three small structures in the woods. Two are slabwood lean-tos with canvas roofs. One protects my old walking tractor from the weather. The other shelters a desk where I write on warm days. The third structure is a camper I've converted into a kind of cabin where I can work year round. All are nestled neatly into the woods. None is visible from the road.

What is visible from the road is a clearing in the north corner of the acreage where a previous owner planned to build a house. Slowly, with much labor, I am encouraging the woods to reclaim the opening. Over the years, I have spent many hours cutting back briars to allow the sun to reach the new growth trees—poplars, cherries, and red maples—I've planted. Though the line marking the old woods remains unmistakable, my labor shows also; ten-foot saplings wave over about a third of the clearing.

This spring I placed a row of bluebird houses along the fence line dividing my land from the horse pasture just north of it. As I walked in this morning, a movement at the farthest house caught my eye. I raised my binoculars and watched. A female bluebird, so softly blue she looked almost gray above her rusty breast, was perched on the roof. A slip of grass in her beak, she leaned over the edge, dropped suddenly to the hole, and disappeared inside. I did not go near. I came here to my desk and began to work. From above me a crazy chirring, nearly a cackling, erupted. The sound was familiar; I had heard it often but had never been able to find its maker in the dense canopy of summer. In the openness of the late budding ash I saw the bright head and striped back of a red-bellied woodpecker.

I put my work aside and sat reflecting. The bluebird and the woodpecker were new—I'd never seen them on Remnant Acres before—but neither was the first new bird I saw this morning. The first was a tom turkey strutting about the hayfield across from the woods. He lifted high one leg and then the other, as if disdaining to touch the dew-damp ground beneath the matted clumps of grass. When he saw me standing beside the car, he broke into a loping run, then launched himself into the air. But he did not fly. Instead, he settled into an effortless glide barely two feet above the contour of the hill, and drifted into the protecting trees a quarter mile away.

Memories of moments like these have made Remnant Acres a storied place for me. So many small things have happened here. Without trying, I have learned so much. For example, it is a wonder to me that on a sunny April afternoon I can push back my chair, say to myself, "The bloodroot ought to be out," and walk to a particular ash beyond the R. G. & E. power line and find at its feet a carpet of small white flowers. It is an equal wonder that minutes ago, after writing that sentence on this May afternoon, I wandered back to the hillside above the spring that is a source of my brook and found, exactly where I expected it to be, a jack-in-the-pulpit. The jack-in-the-pulpits were not here the first year I owned the land. They appeared the year after a Davie Tree crew cleared the right-of-way under the power line.

I wasn't happy about that. They dropped every tree that might ever grow to threaten the uninterrupted flow of power twentieth-century life requires. That incident too is part of the story of Remnant Acres. It is also part of a larger story involving not only these woods, but the earth itself.

The Davie Tree crew appeared in my woods the summer of 1988. When they left I had an uninterrupted view from one side of the wood lot to the other and a long pile of slash to be cut up for the wood stove. The power line, however, is strung over a spring-dotted hillside too wet to work most of the year. Consequently, I did not begin firewooding until midwinter when the ground was frozen and snow covered. On a cold, overcast day I began. I chose to work quietly without the chainsaw. The sharp whack of my axe, the occasional burst of breath as I heaved a four-foot section of log onto my shoulder, and the brisk crunch of my boots breaking through the hard crust of snow were the only noises. I should have been pleased. The day was ideal, but as I walked up and down under the power line, I labored under a shadow that looms over me still.

The night before I had read a chapter from Nick Lyons' *Bright Rivers: Celebrations of Rivers and Fly Fishing*. Lyons, reflecting on life in a Catskill cabin, writes, "Here I can choose as much of the modern world as I want to partake in my life and exclude the rest. There is no fallacy in taking some, in riding the railroad rather than allowing it to ride you. The electric light does me no harm; it enables." As the woodpile I was building grew, I thought of Lyons' words and wished I could be as easy about the light as he was. But I could not. I worked in another world.

In December 1988, a week before Christmas, New York State designated the part of Caneadea east of the Genesee River, along with the adjoining towns of Granger, Allen, West Almond, and Ward, as a candidate site for the state low-level nuclear waste dump. Working in 1989, I knew, as Lyons could not, that the light could do me great harm, for the power surging over my head, the power lighting the horse barn up the road and my house six miles away was generated by a nuclear reactor.

I slogged up and down the line thinking. I had already started attending meetings to discuss possible responses to the news. No one wanted the dump. But the charge of NIMBY ("Not In My Back Yard") hung in the air. The official reasoning went: *Federal law mandates a dump. It must go somewhere. You benefit. Now do your part for the good of all.* On the surface the reasoning seemed irrefutable, obvious, and fair. As I worked that day, however, I came to believe that the reasoning was false; that the reasoning was nothing more than a blind to obscure the real issue, the irresponsibility of the nuclear industry.

Growing out of the Atoms for Peace program, the nuclear industry developed in the mist of a government sponsored euphoria that never allowed the public to consider the true cost or the risk of nuclear power. What the public heard was, *Energy too cheap to meter.* Any question about the disposal of wastes were swept away with the assurance, *The technology is being worked on.* The technology is still being worked on. The technology does not exist. Meanwhile, radioactive waste continues to accumulate. In 1983 commercially generated materials being held in temporary storage facilities in the United States contained over 11 billion curies of radioactivity. That is enough to kill every inhabitant of the country. By the end of the century, the total is expected to reach 42 billion curies—enough to kill every inhabitant of the earth.

This legacy and the inevitable destruction of the productivity of the earth that follows from it is the true cost of nuclear energy. It is the cost the industry is unwilling to pay. It is the cost the public was never asked to approve.

It is no wonder that when the representatives of the New York State Low-Level Nuclear Waste Siting Commission visited Allegany County they wanted to talk about nuclear medicine. Grandma's likelihood of developing cancer, they wanted us to think, was heavy on their minds, and they implied—even threatened—that if we did not accept the dump, Grandma's condition was grave. It did not seem to be a factor in their thinking that less than one percent of the waste that would come to Allegany County should a dump be built here would come from nuclear medicine. Nuclear medicine was to be the camel's nose in the tent of our resistance.

That day, under the power line, working as I have worked since 1977 to meet my own needs from a husbanded renewable source, I decided that the issue of a nuclear waste dump was not a technical issue; it was a moral issue. And I decided that my stewardship of the earth, my responsibility as a Christian to tend the garden and make it fruitful, required me to stand in opposition to the state.

When I made that decision, I made it in faith. I had no idea what demands it would place on me, what actions it would lead to. That it led eventually to civil disobedience and a confrontation with the New York State Police remains beyond my imagination. Had I known, I would have reneged. I would have stayed home and hidden. But I did not know, so one decision at a time, I joined with my neighbors from around the county to do what we believed right.

In early 1990 I was invited to contribute an essay on Lent to a collection of pieces on the church year. My idea was to meditate through Lent on the theme of the redemption of creation. I began a journal and I began to read the Psalms. The events of my life and the words of the psalmist connected. Day after day I set down my words—too many words for a short chapter. And day after day I felt myself drawn into a process from which the only way out was through.

For most readers the narrative line running through the following pages will reach a climax on April 5. It is a climax I am still trying to understand.

Some parts of it are easy. That the police ultimately retreated giving a kind of victory to the local citizenry is not surprising. They were greatly outnumbered and far from support. That the governor called off further attempts to visit the sites and sent the siting process underground is not surprising. He'd tried that before. That all charges against the demonstrators were dropped is not surprising. They existed only for intimidation. Each of these developments was predictable.

What I cannot comprehend is what it all means. Where are we now in this county as a people? What is happening in the siting process? How have I been changed as a result of my participation?

Where we are as a people I cannot say. For a short while (in some very bad weather) we stood together; the differences of class, education, occupation, and faith transcended in devotion to a common cause. I think we are closer today than we were before the dump threatened us. But how long apart from a common enemy that closeness can hold, no one can answer.

Unfortunately no one needs to answer; the common enemy still threatens. After its most recent meeting, the Low-Level Nuclear Waste Siting Commission released a timetable for its work. For the next two years, from now until May 1993, the commission will devote itself to determining a storage methodology. Meanwhile, to satisfy federal law, the state will initiate a program for temporary storage. During this time the commission also plans a series of public presentations explaining itself. Then they will return; they insist the dump site will be selected from one of the five currently proposed sites.

For myself, I am tired of thinking of enemies. I am tired of thinking of myself as a protester, for a protester—though he resists evil—only holds it back. His actions are necessary, but he makes nothing new. He acts neither creatively nor redemptively. If my actions resisting the dump have any meaning, that meaning is found in the link between my protest and the disciplines of my daily life. I am a husband, father, teacher, gardener, and writer. In each of these roles I am a kind of lover and nurturer. I give myself to someone or something other than myself to bring into the world healthy relationships. This giving is redemptive, for its source is the sacrifice of Christ who yielded His position in heaven to enter creation and by His death restored to the Father all that had been lost by our unfaithfulness. For myself the value of my actions lies in my heightened consciousness of the presence of Christ in His world. By His grace I live. And by His grace I live to be a steward of His creation.

Standing Ground

Lent 1990

Ash Wednesday

Today it is bitter cold on Remnant Acres. The temperature is not so low, but a hard wind sweeps across the field from the northwest and swirls the snow into drifts. Because I have been away, my cabin has been unattended for a week. When I came in, carrying my little propane heater, the thin film of ice that forms in the low spot of my writing table was larger than usual. I could not begin to write until I thawed it and wiped it up with a towel I keep for that purpose.

The regular appearance of that sheet of ice (which on warm days is a puddle of water) disturbs me, for I cannot find its source. To all appearances my cabin is tight. I've caulked at least twice every crack I can find. Still the water, insistent and insidious, finds its way in and waits in the center of my table to disrupt my work. What is maddening is that the trail that should allow me to follow the water to the leak has always evaporated.

Today, as I waited for the ice to melt, I saw the water as an analogy for the way sin finds the hidden cracks in my life, flows to the center of my work, and disrupts my relationships with people and with the creation. That is a good analogy to consider on Ash Wednesday, for an awareness of sin and a determination to be cleansed are the order of this day. But since the passing of my adolescence, I have never been able to focus long on my evil nature, nor on any particular acts of either omission or commission. I live rather in the awareness of my redemption, of the work of restoration Christ is doing in me and in creation.

Almost as soon as I drew the analogy of sin infiltrating like water, my imagination leaped ahead to another: Christ, the living water, infiltrating, coming on His own even when we are unaware, uninviting, to bring life to the land. These woods I love are filled with springs. In a few weeks the thaw will come, and everywhere I walk I will walk in water.

March 1

Eight below this morning. When I came into the cabin, my chair was frozen to the floor where the snow had melted from my boots yesterday. To keep warm I have my heater under the table. My legs feel as if I'm standing over a fire, but the rest of me is just about comfortable. That probably has something to do with the insulated underwear and down vest I have on under my sweatshirt. As I sat here thinking about the day, I saw a bit of yellow plastic hanging from my pocket. I pulled on it and drew out an eighteen-inch strip of ribbon, an ACNAG support ribbon.

Allegany County Non-violent Action Group (ACNAG) is just one of the groups organized to oppose the siting of a nuclear waste dump in this poor, sparsely populated county in New York. Ten months ago when the group formed, I thought it wrongheaded, or at least wrong for me. I thought then that the mounting of scientific evidence (trust in experts) and appeals to the judicial system (belief in good intentions and justice) were appropriate. What I have seen since then has changed my mind. Scientific evidence has been ignored or explained away. Conflicts of interest have been revealed. And justice has been abandoned like an infant in a dumpster.

Recognizing this, members of ACNAG have chosen to act directly to halt the siting process until legal remedies can be enacted. Three times now, by using roadblocks and accepting arrests, members of ACNAG have denied the siting commission access to the proposed sites. Each time I have been there not as a potential arrestee but as a support person. I have carried coffee, have helped coordinate communication, and have worked crowd control. So far, arrestees have been charged with disturbing the peace, a violation. Most have pleaded guilty and have been fined $5.00 plus court costs. A few, however, have pleaded innocent and demanded a trial to argue the justness of their cause. I expected to attend one of those trials last night, but it was postponed because of new developments. Last week, a New York State Supreme Court justice granted a blanket injunction against anyone interfering with the siting process. The cost of defending the earth has suddenly risen. The penalty now for contempt of court is up to $1000 in fines and thirty days in jail. The chairman of the New York State Low-Level Radioactive Waste Siting Commission is predicting that the threat of greater fines will end what he calls "the protests."

He is wrong.

The greater cost has forced me to reconsider my involvement. For years I have been writing about the earth, about the Christian responsibility to hold the earth against Christ's coming, to offer it up to Him whole, productive, and healthy. My integrity demands that I stand behind the words I have written. I can no longer ask anyone else to bear the cost of my commitment. I must bear it myself. From now on I will wear the orange ribbon of one committed to going to jail, if necessary, to prevent the despoliation of the earth. I know, as I make this decision, I am not alone. Five hundred gathered for an ACNAG meeting last Sunday.

March 2

I wrote yesterday that I am willing to go to jail to halt the siting of the nuclear waste dump in Allegany County. This morning as Linda and I sat by the fire finishing our coffee and devotional reading, we drifted into conversation. She confessed to me that she is afraid that her emotions will get the better of her. She said, "Yesterday I was thinking that I understand you have to do this. I understand and support you, but all of a sudden I thought, 'Okay, let him do what he has to, but I'm not going to visit him in jail if he leaves me alone.'" Then she burst into tears.

I do not want to go to jail. None of this is a great adventure to me. I want only to come to Remnant Acres and tend this small plot of earth given over to my stewardship. I want to cull deadwood for my fire and plant trees. I want to restore the earth and make it fruitful. Going to jail frightens me. I need open spaces and privacy. Neither will exist in jail, and even thirty days without the touch of my wife, the laughter of my daughter, and the comfort of this good place is appalling to consider.

My thoughts turn to this season, and I see Christ in the garden praying. He did not want to be crucified. His prayer was no easy formality prayed to teach us to yield our wills. It was a struggle equal in intensity to the temptation in the desert. And He said yes to what He knew was coming. He said yes before He knew if *He* had the strength to bear the consequences of His yes.

That is the way we too must say yes when the time for our sacrifice approaches.

I see also Peter beside the fire challenged to identify himself with Christ. And I see him fail. I taste in my mouth his words, "I do not know Him." And I feel rising in me, like the sour aftertaste of too much food, the desire to say, "I don't have to do this. Let someone who sees it as an adventure pay the cost." And I know, precisely because I do not see it as an adventure, because I see it and know it as a sacrifice, that it is mine to pay.

And I pray for the cup to be removed.

March 3

Teaching is supposed to be an occupation filled with joy. The ideal of being present at the awakening of young minds, of fostering intellectual and spiritual growth is ever before me. At times I have felt that joy. Some of my students have blossomed, and I am grateful to have been part of their lives. But more often I feel an emptiness where that joy should be. When I returned to the classroom two months ago after my sabbatical, I was fresh and eager. Each student facing me seemed an opportunity, and I wanted to offer that student myself. I still do. But already the reality is weighing on me.

I can only offer. The student must accept, and few do. Two loom before me. The first is a freshman, an American girl, raised in another culture. She does not want to write. The first day of class she told me she hated writing. Gently, I told her that was okay by me. Not everyone needs to be a writer, though everyone needs to acquire the skills to understand and be understood. She sits in class a stolid lump of passive resistance that chills my soul. Surprisingly, she has done well. In conference I tried to encourage her. I asked, "Having done so well, do you find the class a little more to your liking than you expected?"

She answered in one word, "No."

The second is a senior, an international student, who wants to write. This student has taken her courses out of sequence and hasn't developed the skill to perform at the required level. She is failing badly. And I do not know what to do. How do I tell her she probably hasn't the talent to ever succeed? How do I take from her her dream? Knowing myself, I will probably never tell her. I will probably struggle through the rest of the course suggesting things to her she cannot do, and I will fail her, just as I will fail the freshman who hates to write. Make no mistake, both students will pass; I, the teacher, will fail as I almost always do.

How much easier it is to sit here in my woods putting words on paper, reflecting, and being wise, than it is to teach!

First Sunday in Lent

As I stare at this page, I stare not only at the emptiness waiting to be filled, I stare at the text of an old poem disappearing from the bottom up as the page rolls into the typewriter. The poem is a stupid one. Irrational, pseudo-surreal images that were the fashion fifteen years or so ago when I wrote it. It is good to see it disappear, to see it covered over with new thoughts. Though I remember mailing it out, I'm glad it was never published. The curious thing is that once it was a fair image of me. I thought that way and was proud of it.

I wonder if one day I will look back on the work I'm doing now and feel the same displeasure. Part of me rebels at the thought. I like to think I've matured, that I am now doing good work, work that will stand. And yet I know that all my righteousness (good deeds and good poems) is as a filthy rag, that one day all will be recreated by Christ and made into what He intended creation to be before the Fall.

Meanwhile I have this world with its mixture of good and evil to live in and be a redemptive presence in. I have, in fact, before me the task of being part of the church, the presence of Christ to this fallen world, the task of contributing to that very recreation I await.

To that end I spent this afternoon at an ACNAG training session, speaking to nearly sixty people about the history and principles of non-violent civil disobedience. I was filmed and my mug was displayed on the news as I encouraged people to resist the siting commission.

March 5

It seems strange to be thinking so consciously about Lent. Even in church yesterday, at the Houghton Wesleyan Church, Mike preached on Lent being a time of reflection. He spoke of how when he was a boy, Lent was something Catholics did. And I remembered my boyhood. Since my mother left the Catholic Church when she married my father, my boyhood was filled with mysterious Catholic-Protestant conflicts. I'd visit my cousins and they would talk about the "sisters" at their parochial schools in ways that conjured up images of furies wielding yardsticks and tongues like serpents. It was a world I could neither enter nor imagine; my teachers were all beautiful and kind, and my school days, though lonely, were never frightening. Once a year my cousins would talk about Lent. They'd ask me what I was giving up, and I'd have no answer. They'd tell me they were giving up meat, or their fathers were giving up beer, their mothers candy, and every time we'd meet until the end of the season, they'd tell me how they couldn't wait to sink their teeth into whatever it was they'd given up.

I understand now what it was supposed to mean. I have even on occasion considered trying some sort of observance of sacrifice on my own, but outside of a liturgical framework, it seems an affectation, so I have not.

Yet, this season, I feel as if I have accepted a burden, and in accepting it have given up an element of freedom and a kind of carelessness, the kind practiced by the lilies of the fields. I have given this up in order to direct my thoughts and actions more specifically to the stewardship of the earth. But that isn't quite right. I have for many years been directing my thoughts that way, that is what I did in *In Season and Out;* that is what I have been doing writing the poems for *Country Labors.* What has changed is the overtly political nature of my involvement, my choice to stand, not only in the daily disciplines of my life against the destruction of the earth, but also to stand in the public arena against the marshalled power of destruction. The burden I bear now is the possibility of penal consequences. Yet I dare not retreat.

March 6

Keeping a journal while I was on sabbatical was a joyous, liberating thing. When I read it now, I am filled with the sense that something important was happening; I was finding out about myself; I was making daily discoveries. Continuing this journal, however, depresses me. Two things hang over me like dark clouds cutting off the light. First is the nuclear dump and my sense that I am obsessed by it. It angers me that I cannot let it go, that I cannot patiently trust the Lord, that I feel a need to be always doing something. Even meditating on the theme of creation's redemption only takes me to ranting—the redemption of creation cannot be equated with stopping the dump, stopping the consuming drive of our selfish economy. Second is my constant awareness that these pages are commissioned, that they are going to be read; I keep wanting to impress you, make points, to say important things. That desire keeps me from making discoveries. All I can do is type on, plod across the page, word after word, and hope that in spite of myself something will be said.

I've been reading Eugene H. Peterson's new book on the Psalms, *Answering God.* Last evening his words directed me to Psalm 4, an evening prayer. I read first Peterson's words, "What is wrong with the world is God's business. It is a business in which you will have a part, come morning when you get your assignment. Meanwhile, God is giving help at a far deeper level than any of your meddling will ever reach."

Then I read from the psalm, "I will both lay me down in peace, and sleep: for thou, Lord, only makest me dwell in safety." I went to bed, I prayed, on my back staring into the darkness, and I slept, for the first time in many nights, without dreaming of the dump.

This morning, as I sit here in the quiet of Remnant Acres, I am conscious that I live not only in this world, but in Christ. He is my dwelling place. And I think on what that means. It does not mean that the dump does not matter. Christ is in His creation, and I dwell in Him here, in this world. Here I act out the terms of my salvation. I work it out with fear and trembling. But it is Christ working in me that sanctifies my actions. It is indeed Christ acting when I set my obtrusive, self-conscious self aside. And that changes everything.

I have nothing to do but to choose to be faithful, to offer myself, prepared for whatever Christ desires. To place my body on the arrest line. To write these words. To withdraw. To be silent. To discern the moment when it comes. To refuse to worry until then.

*   *   *

Twice a week the Houghton Church provides a van and driver to chauffeur senior citizens to a county nutrition site for meals and fellowship. Over the summers I enjoy driving the van. Many of the riders are over eighty, a couple are over ninety, and they always enlarge my outlook and enrich my appreciation of life. Sometimes, during breaks in the school year, I fill in if the regular helpers are unavailable. Today was one of those days. The regular helper was available only in the morning. So I went to the nutrition site to make the return trip.

Therein was the problem; I did not know who was on the van. I had only a number, and when that number boarded for a ride home, I thought the load was complete and we left.

Forty-five minutes down the road, one of the ladies asked, "Where's Margaret?"

After several phone calls, I went to Margaret's house. One of the site volunteers had driven her home. She met me gruffly, and I could only say, "I'm sorry." It wasn't my fault, but it was my responsibility. How often it is like that in this world.

March 9

I've been thinking about enemies.

Recently, in response to some comments of mine, a friend wrote about a mutual acquaintance, "I know he's a nice inoffensive man and I've no reason to dislike him, except, of course, that he is my natural enemy and I've no reason, but for the grace of God, to tolerate his existence in the same room." The sentence both delighted and shocked me. I was delighted by its outrageousness and shocked by its accuracy.

I think of myself as a man without enemies. My friend's sentence made me recognize that it isn't so. To the extent that I am Christ's man in this world, I must learn that the enemies of Christ are my enemies. And I must learn to name them enemies. I must do that before I can learn to love them, and loving them I am sure is not at all like loving my neighbors.

Eugene Peterson talks about hate in the context of holiness in the Psalms. He writes,

> We see clearly what we never saw before, the utter and terrible sacrilege of enemies who violate a good creation, who brutalize women and men who are made, every one of them, in the image of God. There is an enormous amount of suffering epidemic in the world because of evil people. The rape and pillage are so well concealed in polite language and courteous conventions that some people can go years without seeing it. And we ourselves did not see it.

Too often I confuse holy with nice, and I choose niceness. I lack the rage of a prophet, of an Amos or a Hosea. We in the Church of the Sanitized Word have become like the patrons of art who consider a Van Gogh on the wall status but a Van Gogh in the family hell.

Well, I can no longer praise tolerance. I have enemies and in no particular order I list them: men who rape children, artists who defend porn and call it freedom of expression, pharisaical Christians who censor art, corporations who elevate profit over health, advertisers who sell their products. R. J. Reynolds. Exxon. Gulf Western. People who drive drunk. Teachers who lie. The nuclear-power industry, which destroys the earth for its stockholders.

Politicians willing to protect the wealthy on Long Island from the health hazards of the nuclear industry. Politicians unwilling to lift a finger to protect the poor and powerless of Allegany County from the same hazards. The siting commission, which hides behind an unjust law and imposes on us the anxiety and hardship of opposing it ourselves. A judge who has ruled in favor of power and turned the judicial system into an instrument of harassment.

Abortionists who make no distinctions. Right-to-Lifers who have no compassion. City officials who close the churches and railroad terminals to the homeless (in the name of safety) on sub-zero nights. The producers of vapid television sitcoms that pander to the basest fascination with sex. Women who sell their body parts for public viewing. Men who delude women and pay them for their humiliation. The food-processing industry and grocery chains that have destroyed the health of a people. Agri-business executives (and fence-to-fence farmers) who have destroyed the health of the soil and our ability to feed ourselves. And many more.

March 10

Today I found the leak in my cabin. It rained as I worked and I followed the tiny trickle of water to the edge of the table. I knelt down and looked up under a small ledge and discovered a nail coming through from outside—a wick. No wonder I could not find it before. How wet it must get before it begins to draw. Yet once it starts how efficiently it pours water across my table.

Second Sunday in Lent

We had in church this morning a time of intercessory prayer when anyone with a special concern could go to the altar to pray and then remain through the pastoral prayer. Knowing that the confrontation with the siting commission (our violating the injunction) will occur on Thursday, I went forward. Were it not for the weeks of prayer and fasting engaged in by the church last fall as we considered our responses to the nuclear dump, I do not believe I could have come to the depth of commitment I have come to. And I do not believe I can sustain it apart from continued prayer—mine and others'.

As I knelt I imagined the faces of as many arrestees as I could call up and held them before God. I prayed for their safety, for their faithfulness, for their resources to maintain the non-violent commitment. And I prayed for the police who will be called upon to enforce the injunction. Then I ceased to make petitions. I fell silent inwardly.

The words of the pastor began to reach me, and I heard him pray for a family whose son had died last night, and I was stunned. The son had been a classmate of my daughter, Melissa, for thirteen years. From the time he was in kindergarten, we had watched him and his family struggle with his muscular dystrophy. And now it had taken him. Disease. Mortality. A young man who never knew the strength of his youth.

Though I hurt and tears threatened my eyes, I also felt a release. And I saw for an instant that young man healed. I saw him leaping in the full glory of the resurrection. Then I fell back into the nearsightedness of my everyday vision—"One world at a time," said Thoreau, it's as much as we can manage—and I saw the grief, the long, slow letting go before the family. And I knew my helplessness in the presence of death. And I knew that the death facing me was more than the death of one young man. I knew it was the death of all creation; a death made possible by our ever failing imagination.

As I prayed, the sound of the organ worked slowly into my consciousness. I began to connect words to the tune. I was praying for the healing of the earth and the words that came to me were, ". . . And the things of the earth will grow strangely dim in the light of His glory and grace." What irony! Oh, I know the intent of the words, the truth they reach after. But I know also their falseness, the abuse they have permitted, and the approbation they have brought on the church. Words count. We dare not sing less than the whole truth. In the light of the glory and grace of Christ the things of this world are transfigured; they are filled with His glory and grace. And so are we.

March 12

No heater today. The temperature is nearly 70 degrees, and the thaw is upon us. For the first time since October, I can see the white pine seedlings I put in the ground. And as I walk across the meadow I can see and hear the water running under the leaves and the grass. Black capped chickadees (which stay all winter) are present in droves, and we have heard and seen the geese returning.

The clearing about the cabin is a mess. Water pools in every low spot. It can neither run off nor sink into the ground until the frost is completely out. The layer of twig-fall catches at my feet as I walk, and sodden piles of ugliness, the black scars of winter fires built in front of the lean-to instead of in the fire pit, mar the ground. Before I started to write, I built a fire in the fire pit, heaped it high with dead pine branches and then began drying and burning off the mess. It probably isn't something that needs to be done. I could just as easily wait for the sun to dry things out sometime in May or June, and then clean it up easily. But that would mean looking at the mess for two or three months.

This morning Linda and I drove the loop around

the proposed Caneadea dump site. We wanted to look back from the site to fix its location in relation to Remnant Acres clear in our minds. One of the things that depressed us was the condition of the farms contrasted with the surface beauty of the land. Only a few are well kept and working. Many are run down, worn out, and nearly useless. One needn't be astute to know that were they factors in the economy of the state the commission would not be lusting after them. What they need are good husbandmen, men and women to love them intelligently rather than mindlessly. The buildings need to be restored or taken down. The fields need to be grassed and healed. The woodlots need to be thinned and protected from logging. The streams need to run free for years to cleanse themselves of fertilizers, pesticides, and herbicides. Part of Adam's task in tending the garden was, I'm sure, tending to its health and beauty, not just its productivity for human enrichment. He was never given permission to discard part of the garden and then move on. And that, by definition, is what a nuclear dump is—an intentional discarding of part of creation.

March 13

Again, no heater. The water on the path is deeper as the frost rises and floods the woods. The cabin door is open and sunlight streams onto the floor and warms my right side as I sit typing. I have read three psalms to the trees and to the Lord, and now I wait for words.

Waiting for them, I encounter my growing reluctance to reveal myself. People who have read *In Season and Out* approach me and say, "I feel I know you so well." When they say that, I feel invaded. I want to say, "No you don't. You only feel. You don't know me at all." And they don't.

The art of keeping a journal is a fictive art, a kind of deception, a selective honesty that guards and protects the writer from being known. Being known is too fearsome to risk. Most of the time we do not even want to know ourselves, let alone be known by others. What is it we fear in God if it is not His ability to know us? Adam's first impulse was to hide himself. It has been our impulse ever since. Is it sin? As I wrote that question, the wind blew my door shut closing off the light of the sun.

Perhaps it is. Perhaps it is the desire to hide from others, from ourselves, and from God a truth we must deny. We are by nature fallen. Even there I hide. I started to write "by nature evil," and I edited as I approached the word *evil*. "Fallen" sounds so much more manageable. A fallen person can be lifted up, can sometimes lift himself up. But an evil person is an evil person. I can accept fallen. It fits into my scheme and understanding of redemption as restoration. Evil doesn't. Evil is too harsh, too total, too final.

How did I get to this point in this morning's writing? Let me go back. Self-revelation. God reveals Himself to us. What He has to hide is only His glory from which He must protect us. This is what T. S. Eliot meant when he said, "Mankind cannot bear too much reality." We reveal ourselves to each other. Our revelations occur in actions and words (which are actions—bursts of air over larynx and tongue— physical manifestations). What glory we have to reveal is not ours, however; it is the glory of God present in us. Clouding that is our own brokenness, our meanness, our ambition, our hatred, which we try to obscure both deliberately and reflexively.

I'm still not getting where I want to go. Where I want to go is a place where there are no words. My only way to get there is through words. I'm a writer, and I have a sense that the end of writing (the purpose) is to go without words. Few of my friends believe me when I say that someday I'm going to stop writing and that I long for that day. I'm going to get there, to that place, to that time. It may kill me. I may have to die, but I will get there.

The art of writing is the art of entering silence, of coming to an end that launches one.

There are, however, false silences along the way that one dare not rest in. These silences must be denied. They occur when people say, "I feel I know you so well," and you know that the one they know is false. Then one must babble on as I do now.

I want to quit, now and forever. I want to end

this entry. I want to end this journal. I am too much with me. Filled with self, I am weightless and foolish.

What writing have I done that approaches silence? A few poems. The end of *Nightwatch*. What do I want for the rest of my life? Only to approach silence again and finally to enter it unencumbered by the obligation of reporting back to anyone.

The selfishness! Or as Conrad wrote, "The horror!"

March 14

I've been talking about the upcoming civil-dis-obedience action as a burden. One day I compared it to the cup Jesus prayed to have removed in the garden. For the moment the cup seems to have been removed. Sunday at the ACNAG steering committee meeting I learned that the commission planned to make its assault on the West Almond site. Because my duties as a monitor require me to stay at the Caneadea site no matter where the action occurs, I felt a relief. Most likely—unless the arrests reached the hundreds—I would spend the day in relative isolation, keeping my post with a few others. "They also serve who only stand and wait." Only a sudden change of plans on the part of the commission could put me at risk.

Still I faced that action, scheduled for tomorrow,

with much anxiety. Watching from a distance has its own tensions. Then last evening I received a call—the action was off. The commission would not come. The paper said that the sheriff had advised against it at this time. I wondered what was what.

This morning, as I drove to an 8:00 A.M. admissions meeting, I listened to the news and was startled and angered to hear the commission chairman quoted saying that they would not come because of a small group threatening violence. I know of no such group. His statement is simply another sound-bite designed to influence public opinion, another ploy to paint his opposition black, another maneuver to portray himself as an innocent public servant struggling to do his duty. I'm finding it increasingly difficult to hate the sin and love the sinner. At what point does a sinner become his sin? At what point does the distinction cease to matter?

And what does this news mean? Does it mean that perhaps the commission is recognizing that they have so poisoned the waters in Allegany County that they will never site a dump here; that they are returning to Albany (I know their office is in Troy, but their spiritual home is Albany) to find an alternative to confrontation, a new plan for storage? Or does it mean more days and weeks (months) of tension and building emotion while they seek other ways to impose themselves on the rural population?

And what does it mean to me as a Christian? How am I to be a peacemaker when every day my anger grows and my ability to moderate my emotions decreases? How am I to deal with the nightmares that come to me when I sleep? What do I do with that streak in me that finds it hard to care about the safety of the commission?

March 15

Another day I'm not being arrested. I'm at Remnant Acres as usual, but a little early, so the sun has not reached round enough to enter the door to warm the cabin. I've built a small fire and I sit beside it at my outdoor table. The fire is more for bug protection than heat. Another day of record warm temperatures is predicted. These days are beautiful, but they must end before they bring out the dogwood and apple buds prematurely. For a moment last night, when I looked out onto the street before going to bed, I thought, *I'm going to miss the snow, the close comfort of the wood stove.* I'm also going to enjoy crisp mornings on the Wiscoy stalking trout, and the crumble of soil in my hands as I put in the garden.

Since the other day, I've been thinking about enemies. Having once introduced them to my thoughts, I can't seem to get rid of them. Yesterday I got a letter from my friend, the distinguished poet, John Bennett. In it he wrote,

> . . . and perhaps you can't write satire because you have not yet become angry

enough. Hate the sin and love the sinner? I can't do that: a grave weakness in my Christian being-ness, I suppose. I hate every son-of-a-bitch who is/works for Exxon. I hate every yapping, howling idiot who sings rock'n roll commercials. I hate the vacuous ad writers who have other vacuous fools gobbling on TV. I hate the predatory homosexual and the rampant feminist harridans (I voted for ERA, and will again). Yep. Perhaps all that makes my satire strong (I think it is) but it also makes me contemptible/unreadable/unacceptable to a society in which what I condemn prevails—blandly, arrogantly, stupidly—and in death.

His list is remarkably similar to mine. And I think of a poem by Samuel Hazo where Hazo says, "I hate fair." I wonder, is tolerance a characteristic of the young? Does the ability to hate come with age? Strange phrasing for a Christian—the ability to hate. Strange thoughts for Lent. I should be confessing my hate and asking forgiveness, and here I am meditating on it, nurturing it. So be it. For the moment. I read in Psalm 5 yesterday morning, "For thou art not a God that hath pleasure in wickedness: neither shall evil dwell with thee. The foolish shall not stand in thy sight: thou hatest all workers of iniquity. Thou shalt destroy them that speak lies. . . . Destroy thou them, O God; let them fall by their own counsels." The psalmist sounds like us. He seems to make no distinctions between sinner and sin either.

There is a sense, perhaps, in which, in practice, we are our actions, in which we are our sins incarnated. (I intuit that sentence. I'm not sure I understand it.) Apart from me, my sins would not exist. By myself I am sin to the world. Redeemed, I am somehow made Christ to the world. Paul, I think, spoke of Christ becoming sin for our sakes. Here, perhaps, is where the twist comes, is where we must learn to encounter our hates and make them somehow redemptive. As Linda and I read evening prayer last night, these words from the intercession stood out to me: "Reward all who have done us good, and pardon all those who have done or wish us evil, and give them repentance and better minds. Be merciful to all who are in trouble; and do thou, the God of pity, administer to them according to their several necessities; for His sake who went about doing good, thy Son our Savior Jesus Christ."

Three things struck me. First the prayer to give those, who would do me evil, better minds. Evil is not just in the heart. It is intellectual and chosen. It can be rejected. Second, those who do evil are in trouble and have needs. The trouble is not so much that they are under the judgment of God, He is merciful and desires them to be whole. The trouble is they reap the consequences of their own actions— they become their sins. And third, our concern in this is Jesus Christ our Savior, who because of all this has become sin. We must become whole for His sake. There is some sense in which He who is whole and complete in Himself in His place in the Trinity, needs also our wholeness, our redemption, and the re-establishment of the order of creation before we chose sin.

Perhaps holy hatred is, like love, relational. Perhaps it is a necessary beginning for valid witness. Perhaps the tolerant are the lukewarm to be spewed out into nothingness, into the nothingness of their own acceptance of evil. Another paragraph in John's letter comes clear. He added a word of caution.

> One cannot hate without regret, or one cannot hate without restraint, or one cannot hate without discrimination, or one cannot hate with enjoyment—else what is hated becomes the hater, the moral trap is sprung, the "good" man becomes subject (deeply subject and oddly subject) to the evil he would oppose. So there is my caveat: don't sentimentally forgive evil, don't (or rarely) turn the other cheek, don't gloss over the fact of the world's murder by industry, by greed, by stupidity, by mindless evil turning natural good to corruption and death. But always be aware, always be very much aware, that the hatred, if it is to be good hatred and morally usable, is really another aspect, side, dimension of love.

March 16

I did not expect to come here today; I expected to spend the morning in my office, but I cannot stay away. I have become dependent on these mornings in the woods to invite my soul, to establish and hold a balance in the whirlwind of activity around me. This morning especially I need . . . I don't know what I need.

Two things weigh on me. One I cannot talk about. What I can't say in particular is how we hurt each other in spite of our claims to be Christians. How we allow our egos, our need to win, to take over a situation and drive us to words that should never be uttered, to cruelties, and to deliberate distortions of others' intent, which in our better moments we would never consider. Then how, after the fact, we justify our words in the name of righteousness. When I began these words I had others in mind. As I write them I know I have done the same thing.

I see in my mind a summer day six or seven years ago when the church youth group (my daughter among them) returned from a mission trip to Haiti. In the Sunday evening service they reported to us. They sang in Creole and then in English,

> "Oh how He loves you and me,
> Oh how He loves you and me,
> He gave his life,
> What more could He do? . . ."

Tears filled my eyes that day as I looked at those kids. How overwhelming it was to know that each loved and was loved. And under this, I think, was a dark unstated consciousness that their lives would never be more beautiful than they were at that moment, that ahead of them waited hurt and loss and grief. All those things have come to them.

What has this to do with the previous thoughts? This: the deep pain, the grief of witnessing sin's dominion in this world, the grief of knowing that sin is in fact defeated, but that the victory is not yet fully ours.

I can talk in particular of the pain of my dreams. I woke this morning to Linda's hand caressing me, and her voice repeating, "It's all right. You're dreaming. Wake up. It's okay." I was sobbing, and though it is hours later—I have prepared my classes, attended a committee meeting on campus, and answered my mail—the mood is still on me. I dreamed my neighbor's child, a small precisely featured child who was born with a cleft palate and has endured surgeries that have made him whole and beautiful, had died. His father is an artist and a craftsman. In my dream he had fashioned him a perfect wooden coffin. I saw the child in memory as he had played in the yard, his beguiling grin, his voice calling me, "Jack." And I saw the box, the work of his father's hands, and I cried out, as I have never cried out in life, "It isn't fair!" And Linda woke me.

And now in life, I think, I am crying out for all the injured, for the hosts about me. "It isn't fair!"

"God, it isn't fair!"

And then the song, "He gave his life . . ." And

that wasn't fair either. How could we do that? How can we do that to Christ?

March 17

Saturday. A day in which little has gone right. Nothing major, no real problems. Just this and that not working out as planned. It was three o'clock by the time I got here, and I was so annoyed I went off to the back of the woods and stacked the three-quarters cord of wood I cut a week ago for next winter.

Both wood burners and teachers live in a time in which the future is part of the present. What I do today, though I do it only for today, determines what will be possible tomorrow. I cannot act for tomorrow, for it remains unknown. I can only act faithfully going about the duties of the day. If—no—whether or not I am faithful, the future will take care of itself.

It rained last night so the woods are soaking wet again. I found a small stack of firewood I set aside last fall when the woods were dry, smack in the middle of a spring runoff. It weighed heavy when I moved it aside, straddling the running water because I haven't boots on, only an old pair of sneakers.

A down day. Enough of nothing.

Were I to go on I think I would become very melancholy, then romantically introspective, then self-hating, and I'm not up to it.

Going to dinner tonight with intelligent, witty friends. I need to force myself out into the midst of people.

Third Sunday in Lent

Mike preached from Colossians this morning. His theme was the necessity of sacrifice to validate one's witness. He kept returning to Paul's imprisonment, to the idea that it was the result and the proof of his faithfulness.

Every time he returned to it, I returned to Allegany County and the nuclear-dump resistance. I have not yet been arrested. Indeed, since the January confrontations, no one has been arrested, for the commission has chosen to stay away. The last week has been entirely peaceful, and I have directed my thoughts to other matters. Still, I have been thinking of sacrifice. I have been thinking of my writing, of the work I do here each morning typing these pages. How do I offer up this work as a sacrifice to God?

I begin with the nature of this work. Part of me does not want to do it; the core of journaling is discovery and revelation. In a journal a writer explores his personhood and his relationships. When he allows the journal to be read, he lets others into his life. He gives away knowledge of himself; he gives others power to invade his privacy. That bothers me greatly, for I am becoming an increas-

ingly private person. My earlier willingness, as a
writer, to reveal myself strikes me as somewhat self-
absorbed and egotistical. I often relate to my students E. B. White's observation that essayists must
believe everything that happens to them is of interest
to everyone else, that essayists are unrepentant
egotists. I usually go on to justify that apparent
egotism on the grounds that if what happens to a
sparrow is of importance to God, what happens to
humans must be of importance to humans. I argue
that all experience is of consequence and that writing
is giving testimony. I think that is true, but I fear it
can only be true of a saint. For the rest of us it is ego.

I have three thoughts going here: (1) writing
about the self is revelatory in a way that makes the
self subject to invasion; (2) writing about the self is
egomania and sin; (3) writing about the self is a way
of giving testimony, of speaking the truth about
one's life.

The testimony is the ideal. It is what writing
about the self reaches after. The necessary revelation,
however, is corrupted by the egomania and the
desire for safety, the desire to remain hidden.

What then does one do? Write on and hope for
the best? Shut up? Frost has a poem called "How
Hard It Is to Keep from Being King When It's In You
and In the Situation." Perhaps, if one is a writer, one
can't shut up. No matter how the writing disturbs
one, how the writing causes anxiety, irritability, fear,
and doubt.

Sometimes I hate being a writer. If I could be reincarnated, I'd choose to be a bear far from human habitation, and I'd eat blueberries all summer, and sleep all winter.

How do I offer this work up as a sacrifice? How can I offer up something I'd like to get rid of? Perhaps there is my answer, or part of my answer. I offer it up by taking it up, by not discarding it. I offer it up by affirming the goodness of the task—recognizing the complexity of motives at work, the testimony and the egomania—by putting aside my desire to sort it all out and be pure in heart or silent, by simply doing it and relying on grace to guide me wherever it will.

By laboring faithfully until someday I wake, in another world, to find myself a saint, one made perfect by the Christ who takes our work and makes it His.

Perhaps it would be easier to go to jail.

March 19

My schedule today is disrupted by other duties. So I arrived anxious and annoyed. Cold has returned, and here on the hill, snow is slowly covering the woods' floor. As I walked in, I noted curious patterns on the ground where trees broke the wind-driven snow and created lines free of snow like shadows on the ground. In the cabin the desk puddle was frozen. I set up my heater under the desk and read psalms out loud until it melted and I regained some equilibrium. Though the psalms are full of talk about enemies, they do not let the psalmist/reader off the hook. I read in my anger at circumstances this morning, "Oh Lord my God, if I have done this; if there be iniquity in my hands; If I have rewarded evil unto him that was at peace with me . . . Let the enemy persecute my soul, and take it."

Some days ago, when I began this journal, I said something about not being able to focus long on my sins, about moving directly to grace and being overwhelmed by it and by the restoration taking place. It seems, however, as I've meditated here, I've turned more and more to consciousness of my own sinfulness. What I wonder this morning is where that will take me. How will it lead me to change my life?

The nature of my sin is not flagrant—I needn't stop gambling, boozing, and womanizing. My sins are more subtle, tied to my virtues, are indeed virtues twisted into tools for my own advancement. But I'm not being quite fair to myself. My sin is not jealousy or ambition. It is a concern for good that fails to contain the good of all in its drive for the immediate good of a few. I'm too small. My emotional range isn't large enough to feel all needs. If I had the range to empathize more broadly, I could comprehend the needs that drive others, the needs that make them act unjustly. Then I could act redemptively rather than vindictively to gain a victory—my own way.

March 20

Reading Thomas Merton this morning I'm finding things that apply to the issue of the dump and civil disobedience. In his conference with the sisters in Alaska, the September before his death in Bangkok, Merton chose to emphasize establishing a climate of peace and trust rather than a climate of agitation and tension. If one cannot act out of peace and love, Merton argues, he should resist acting and wait for the peace of Christ to grow in him and lead him to action. The waiting itself is action.

Applying this to civil disobedience in Allegany County is difficult. How many of the activists are seeking to act out of the peace of Christ? How many of them would even know what I'm talking about? Probably more than I imagine, but I have no way of knowing their hearts, and I should not judge one way or the other. At any rate, I know myself. When I think of the commissioners, when I think of the power companies, when I think of the politicians, I do not have in me the peace of Christ. I have in me the spirit of strife and animosity. It does not matter that I claim to have a justified anger, that I claim to be angry for the sake of the earth. It may be true that intellectually I feel I'm defending the Lord's earth against an oppressor, but emotionally I'm trying to take over the Lord's job and act for Him rather than allowing Him to act in me. Merton writes, "We have not covenanted to give God any great work. We have simply promised that we will listen and that we will believe His promise, and this is terribly important in our life."

Without being fatalistic I must remember that the Lord has risked His creation. He has turned it over to humankind. Scripture tells us that His world in fact is the kingdom of the Prince of Darkness. It should not surprise me that he is seeking to destroy. It should not surprise me that the commissioners insist that the dump go in an unspoiled place. Spoiling the goodness of the earth is the whole point. Powers and principalities reign. They are evil and they seek whom they will destroy.

In all this, however, there is another power, the power of Christ and His Holy Spirit. He is seeking to restore. He has already suffered the destruction of the powers and the principalities on the cross, and He has defeated them. As much as our pride desires it, defeating the commission is not our task.

Practically what does this mean? What must I do? First, I must love. Even the commissioners. This means I must serve the earth not by opposition but by loving faithfulness and example. Should I stand with those who march? Yes. I must reveal my love for them to them, but I must also remember that my love is null should it fail to be inclusive, should it fail to include those we seek to influence. Perhaps that is a clue to how I must act. I must woo the servants of the powers and principalities, I must seek to win them, not defeat them.

The dump is an issue. It is not *the* issue. *The* issue, even here, is love.

March 21

Since Sunday there have been rumors of changes in the LLNW (low-level nuclear waste) siting process. Members of the legislature have been meeting with Governor Cuomo. Yesterday a report on the noon news stated the process was going to be halted, and I, along with some others, had a few hours of euphoria. The evening news, however, dashed all hope. What the governor proposes is to delay the siting process without changing it, allow the same determined commissioners to decide on a method of disposal (something they have claimed to be unable to do without a site), and then return to naming a site at a later date. The genius of this scheme is that it gives the appearance of being responsive to the people, while allowing the same forces presently in the public eye to go behind the scenes and continue their plot against the earth unopposed.

The absolute sinfulness of the process overwhelms me. I want to cry with the psalmist, "Thou shalt destroy them that speak lies; the Lord will abhor the bloody and deceitful man." Surely the governor is aware that his scheme is deceitful. He cannot be so consistently deceptive, slippery, and generally sold out to ambition and power as not to know what he is doing. He may, however, be so self-deceived as to think he is doing a good thing (being responsible about energy needs, serving the bloated god, *Economy*) that he is willing to use any means to achieve his end. Let his end be an early retirement, a rejection at the polls.

*   *   *

The sun is glorious today. I would like the door open to enjoy it, but the air is too crisp; it demands walking. So I sit with the door shut in the gray but adequate light of the cabin.

I have spent so much time wondering if there are any circumstances under which I would accept the construction of a nuclear dump. I have concluded that while the answer is yes, the circumstances are so unlikely as to make the speculation comic. But just for laughs, let me speculate.

Imagine the business and political community attending a joint evangelistic extravaganza featuring Billy Graham and Tony Campolo. First Billy slashes them with the sword of the Lord and cuts the sinfulness from their hearts. He gets them on their knees at the altar pleading for their souls, which of course the Lord in His infinite wisdom and mercy has provided for. But then, instead of sending them off to home churches to go their individualistic ways, Billy returns them to their seats for part two: Tony on social responsibility. Tony, sweating profusely, harangues them with how they haven't shown proper concern for the poor and how, now that they are Christians, that has to change. The Spirit not having departed, works not only the salvation of the mass, but the sanctification of the whole bunch. They are changed.

The next morning they go to their offices bearing in their briefcases a burden for the poor. By 9:01 every phone line in the country is tied up as AT&T, MCI, Sprint, Sprite, and Spurt interface the largest conference call in history. Everyone talks to everyone at once. It sounds like Babel. Only God, instead of confusing their language, grants them understanding. Everyone hears everything. They get Tony on the line. "Tony," they say, "what shall we do?"

"Sell everything and give to the poor," he answers.

"Yea, verily," they reply, "but what in practice does that mean?"

"Well, for starters," Tony suggests, "decentralize energy production. Give people the sun. And don't put a meter on it."

"Whoa!" they answer. "What an idea! It's even a pun. You have given us the Son; now we in response give the sun to others. It's a kind of evangelism. We'll go for it!"

"Great," says Tony. "And now that you don't need all those nuclear reactors that never made anything but profits for your greedy little hearts anyway, what are you going to do about all that radioactive waste you've been giving the earth?"

A roar goes up on the conference line, deafening poor Tony, but it's all right, his mission is done. "We're going to clean it up."

"Wait," says one quiet voice, a politician from a district far from Albany, a politician from a district with almost no people, a politician with a secret membership in The Nature Conservancy. "You can't clean it up. It lasts forever."

Silence falls on the lines.

Finally someone speaks, a director of Niagara Mohawk. "Well, I guess since we made most of it, it's up to us to take responsibility. Perhaps we could gather it all into one place, stabilize it, and watch over it for the thousands of years it will take to ensure the health of the people and the safety of the earth."

The politician from the distant district replies, "That's a generous offer, but what of the place you gather it into. You will be destroying that place."

"I know," the NiMo executive answers sadly. "I'm afraid that is the consequence of sin. Though we are forgiven, we are not freed of what we have done. We must ask another sacrifice. Just as Christ died for us, a part of the earth must die for us. If we are faithful, in thousands of years, it too will rise, and the redemption of the earth, begun by Christ will be finished as He works in us."

Just a fantasy—one I could live with.

March 22

I've been thinking about words and how we use them in our culture. I've been thinking about advertising and the selling of goods. I've been thinking about politics and the use of words to persuade. And I've been thinking about my words in this journal.

I begin with a given—that is an idea from outside, a revelation—Christ is the Word. I do not really know what that means, and I do not think that I can, in fact, ever know what that means. I can, however, draw some meanings from it. Christ identified Himself as "The Way, the Truth, and the Life." I want, for the moment, to think about the connection, the identification between word and truth. If Christ is both word and truth, then, in some sense, in our experience the two are connected. Though they often are not, I take as a starting point for my writing and speaking that the function of words is to connect with truth, that the function of words is first to speak what is, to be descriptive of the truth. All other functions of words grow out of this. If the description fails, then all else fails.

Advertising. Is the word here used descriptively? I think not. In advertising, words are used not to describe accurately, but to affect the hearer, to persuade him to act. Here the end of the word is not an accurate account of reality but a purchase.

Politics. Not only is the connection between word and truth denied in the realm of politics, it is treated as a joke. It is an axiom that a politician cannot speak the truth; he must speak what the public wants to hear or be turned out of office. The public knows this, mocks the politician's lies, and requires him to continue in them. The public, by its use of the politician's words, lies to itself. The politician has become a hired liar, the one who tells us lies about ourselves, so we can avoid truths. We, the public, have made him what he is. We despise him because even in his lies he tells us the truth about ourselves.

Persuasion. When we set out to persuade, we begin with an end in mind. We set out to bend words, to control them, so that they say, not what truth might demand, but what we demand. Yesterday a student came into my office to discuss a paper that argued in favor of heavy-metal music as an evangelistic tool. His goal was to persuade his parents that he was right and they were wrong. No questions I raised about aesthetics, about the relationship of form and content could reach him. I wasn't disagreeing with him (though I do), I was trying to get him to examine his words. He would not; they said what *he* wanted to say and that was truth enough for him.

This journal. How often have I said what *I* wanted to say about the siting commission, about the governor, and found that truth enough for me? I suspect more than once. Yesterday I called the governor a liar. Then I qualified it a little and called him self-deceived. Both may be true, but how do I know? I do not know. Not for certain. The desire to speak prophetically is dangerous. Though we try, the Lord will not let us put words into His mouth. He will, if we let Him, put words in ours.

Most of what I said yesterday was based on what I read in the newspapers. I trusted them to be true. This morning a different paper calls into question the quotations I accepted as true, not quotations from the governor, but quotations from his opponents on the dump issue, the men I trust. Today I learned they claim not to have made the statements attributed to them. Today they challenge the reporter writing them, and credit the false quotations with damaging long, delicate, and profitable negotiations.

How hard it is to speak simply without self-dramatization, without self-inflation. I need to with-hold my violent judgments. I need to learn to speak descriptively, to say only what is and allow the fact of what is to persuade honest hearers.

I told my student that he was using an end, the salvation of souls (he assured me kids are saved at heavy-metal concerts), to justify a questionable means. I told him that he must examine the means.

I must do the same.

All this feeds my desire to turn away from prose writing. For me it is nothing more than a temptation to posturing and grandstanding. Only in my poetry, where my discipline protects me from myself, do I rise above cheap shots and begin to get at the connection between word and truth. Only there do I begin to speak redemptively. Only there do I begin to disappear.

March 23

I dreamed last night that a great controversy raged in Houghton. Toys-R-Us had purchased a plot of land near the college maintenance center and planned to build a large warehouse and distribution center. The community was divided over the project. Some were angry that the building would disturb the pastoral view and atmosphere. Others were furious at the implied insult to an academic community; toys and a backward R!

How I wish that were the issue.

Fourth Sunday in Lent

I did not write yesterday. I forced myself not to, and by evening I was bothered. This project has become obsessive. I want to miss nothing. I had two things in mind when I chose not to write yesterday. First, I simply needed a break, a time to ease the intensity this kind of introspection produces over time. Life gets turned into material. Second, I was upset about a conversation with a friend who supports the nuclear industry. I couldn't yesterday, and I still can't today, sort out how to balance friendship with opposition. Trying to be nonconfrontational, I gave up too much of my commitment to ease the moment. It's easy to call the siting commission to judgment. It's difficult to call a friend to judgment. Friendship is complex. I know my friend is a good man. My friend and I value many of the same things. We part company over how and why we value them. Edward Abbey's line that the belief in growth for growth's sake is the ideology of cancer cells would make no sense to my friend. It is growth that provides comforts. Comforts are good. Don't question what they cost in Third World lives, in ecological damage. Growth/technology will fix it.

What is a friendship worth? How much truth does one sacrifice? What is the cost of peace in our time?

*   *   *

The fourth Sunday in Lent is the halfway point. In his sermon this morning Mike pointed out that traditionally this Sunday is a feast day, a hold in the process of introspection and focus on repentance to remember redemption, to remember Christ and to give thanks. It is a day of celebration.

We celebrated communion.

March 26

Saturday, cutting a large ash tree, I endured several moments of near terror when the tree would not fall though I had cut it nearly through. I was working alone—something no one should do, but something everyone around here does. I had carefully cleared the fall-line of the tree and my escape route. Nothing should have gone wrong. In fact nothing did go wrong, but since I was alone, I was being cautious. When the tree did not fall at the point I thought it should, I looked up the trunk. Sixty feet of ash swayed gently above me, swayed as if it were firmly rooted, not held by a one-inch hinge. "Lord, preserve me," I prayed, and went for help.

Larry looked at the tree and agreed; it should have fallen. So while he watched, I cut some more. The tree cracked slightly. I shut down the saw and stepped back. The tree did not move. "A little more?" I asked.

Larry nodded.

I grabbed the pull rope on the saw, but before I jerked it, the tree gave way. The hinge snapped, and the tree, which had been perfectly balanced, dropped into the wedge I had cut and then toppled to the ground exactly where I'd intended it to hit.

I'd done everything right.

We stood shaking our heads at its stubbornness.

We counted the rings. The tree was forty-six. It began growing the year I was born. I noted a series of tight rings some years back. The tree had suffered some hard years, just as I had, but had weathered them. A dark stain, however, had penetrated to the heartwood from the large wound where the bark had broken away from the trunk. The tree was dying.

I stood, looking down the trunk, and felt my own mortality.

Yesterday, when I came here to write, I could not resist walking out to see the tree. Somehow I expected it to be changed, though I knew it wouldn't be. The day was bright with sunshine, pleasantly cool in the low forties. Without planning, I began to drag some of the thornapple slash that lay about to the brush pile by the fence line. I worked an hour before I returned to writing, and in that time I felt a deep peace and joy. Occasional thoughts about the nuclear dump, about the waste man makes of creation came to me, but in the midst of the work I was doing they could not hold my imagination. The clearing I made, the planting I would do was too hopeful. And I was happy.

I don't have to win against the dump. I have only to be faithful both in my opposition, and in my actions toward this place I love.

March 27

For the first time this Lent I am not writing at the cabin. I am sitting at home, at my old Royal standard with no "Q" key. It feels very strange to be looking out the window through the budded dogwood into the street and to hear Linda in the background. It also feels odd to be looking at the words appearing before me. This typewriter needs to be cleaned, so all the letters are blotted black—no "o's" are open. My portable Smith-Corona in the woods has a worn-out ribbon and types a line as gray as a New York winter sky.

I went out a few minutes ago to get some wood for the fire. The morning is crisp—20 degrees—clear and inviting. I'd like to be in the woods. But I'm also tired. Literally tired, for at 2:00 A.M. last night a neighbor's car horn stuck and sounded for ten minutes before he roused to turn it off. Waking slowly to the strange sound, I took several minutes to identify it. Then I went from window to window trying to locate its source. We live in a hollow where sounds echo and come from everywhere at once. Lights came on in houses around me. People came out into the cold. And then, at last, the owner, bathrobe clad, came out.

Fifteen minutes later it went off again. Again, bathrobe clad, the owner came out. This time I watched him raise the hood and pull the battery cable. I fixed a bagel, had a glass of orange juice, read for a while, and finally returned to sleep around 3:00 A.M.

But that's not the tired that plagues me. What plagues me is a weariness—not in well-doing, though I hope what I am doing is good and right— but a kind of vexation. I rise to moments of joy like those of Sunday, and then I fall into slumps, lethargies, hours of wondering if anything matters; the work of my students is mediocre, the siting commission has gone underground, demographics plague the college, faculty whine. Life goes on—and on.

What gets me is the necessity to will the meaningfulness of dailiness. Its meaning exists apart from our willing; I believe that. But the meaningfulness we experience is the meaningfulness we will and enter into by imagination. And always there is a sense that since the meaningfulness is made, it is inaccurate, not fully true, partly a lie.

What is needed, somehow, is an ability to let go of the made meaningfulness, to float into the meaning not bound by words. There's an old expression around the church, "Let go and let God." It appeals to me and terrifies me. To let go of our words that make the meaningfulness is to release control.

Wait. Even though I'm using words, creating half truths, I am getting at something. Last night I read "When We Dead Awaken," by Adrienne Rich. In it she writes,

> If the imagination is to transcend and transform experience, it has to question, to challenge, to conceive alternatives, perhaps to the very life you are living at the moment. You have to be free to play around with the notion that day might be night, love might be hate; nothing can be too sacred for the imagination to turn into its opposite or to call experimentally by another name. For writing is re-naming . . . the subversive function of the imagination.

The passage made me first uneasy, then angry. I growled from the floor in front of the fire to Linda, read the passage to her, and said, "That's a definition of sin!" This morning I am convinced I am right—it is a definition of sin—but I am not so easy in my roaring, for I think that re-naming is what all too often takes place when we write. We do not name. We do not see accurately (we cannot see accurately for we have been formed in sin) and do not name as Adam named, perceiving the inherent qualities of a thing or an experience. We see rather the distorted. Our seeing distorts and we name/re-name. We play around with notions. We reduce the Word to wordplay, and out of our mouths we issue sin. We make the world sin.

Some days I want to shut up. But that can be an evasion, simply a refusal to accept our task of naming. We must speak—even in our brokenness, accepting what partial truths we can get at, holding none of them too confidently—if only to damn the fall.

March 28

I just finished reading Will Campbell's *Brother to a Dragonfly*. Because ACNAG is engaged in civil disobedience, our resistance is often compared to the civil-rights movement. It is not an apt comparison. We personally risk much less than the civil-rights workers, for we have the support of the community in which the action takes place, and we have at least a measure of sympathy from the police officers sent to deal with us.

What likeness exists lies in the common resistance to injustice and oppression. The civil-rights movement resisted injustice to blacks. It has since expanded to resist injustice to all minorities. If one is able to imagine the creation a minority (one disenfranchised to be used), we are part of the civil-rights movement. For most, however, that is a little much to imagine. Our concerns are generally human centered, and what one hears most often in Allegany county is resistance to the land seizure involved in the siting process.

In all this I struggle with how I love the land because it is the creation of the Lord and how I love those who, while bearing the image of God, abuse the creation. I am called to do both. Individuals and creation cry out for redemption. As the messenger of the Good News, I must articulate the full vision.

If I could separate the good guys from the bad guys, if I could say with certainty that the officers of the siting commission, the politicians, and the representatives of the growth-for-growth's-sake industries were all evil, then I could simply call down fire. I could claim love requires a prophetic voice—repent or else. But I cannot in my best moments indulge in such reductionism. That way masks anger. It allows for self-deception.

All I have written about holy hatred leaves me unconvinced. It may be true in the abstract. But it is not true in me; my hatred is simply anger. I may on occasion (in writing a poem) transcend my anger to speak prophetically, but I do not transcend my anger in my daily attitudes.

That way also obscures my relationships with others who make the work of the nature abusers possible. These others are friends who will not discipline their lives to do with less, who will not see that their comfort comes at the expense of something—other humans, nature, the future. In these others I must include myself, for I profit daily. One friend said it all. He looked at my "No Nukes" button (a small tasteful button) and said, "That's wrong, you know. Your electricity comes from a nuclear plant."

Will Campbell's book helps me with this. Challenged to give a ten-word definition of Christianity, Campbell answered in eight, "We're all bastards but God loves us anyway." Later when a civil-rights worker is murdered, the definition comes back to haunt him. The same man who goaded him into the definition applies it. "Which of these two bastards does God love the most? Does He love the little dead bastard, [the murdered worker] Jonathan, the most? Or does He love the living bastard, [the murderer] Thomas, the most?"

The whole point of redemption, the whole point of God's love, is that the two will be/are reconciled. Justice is blown away by grace. Jonathan and Thomas eat the same supper, the same body of the Lord.

I don't find this easy. Such grace offends me. I want to cry like a child, "It isn't fair!" And I realize that my only hope is its unfairness. I am not humbled, I am humiliated. My rage is shown for what it is, and I repent.

What I don't understand is what, after I have repented, I must do.

Campbell's reflections help. He wrote,

> I had become a doctrinaire social activist, without consciously choosing to be. And I would continue to be some kind of social activist. But there was a decided difference. Because from that point on I came to understand the nature of tragedy. And one who understands the nature of tragedy can never take sides. And I had taken sides. . . . We did not understand that those we so vulgarly called "redneck" were part of the tragedy. They had been victimized. . . . They had their heads taken away by cunning, skillful and well educated gentlemen and ladies of the gentry.

He is talking about the way the economically vulnerable whites had been manipulated into hating the blacks to the advantage of a social system. Recognizing this, he began going not only to the blacks with the gospel of reconciliation, but to the rednecks, to the Klan.

I can learn from his example. "We are all bastards but God loves us anyway." I own a house, a nice comfortable house. It is heated half by wood I cut myself, half by natural gas. My electricity is generated by a nuclear reactor. I have two credit cards, and I owe money on both of them. I own a car, and I put lots of miles on it. I am a white, middle-class consumer. A bastard. God loves me anyway. In response to that love, I seek to love not only the creation that I have a natural inclination to love, but those I live and work with. Love requires that I see their victimization by the system of economic and social oppression that they apparently profit by. Love requires me to see that that profit is an illusion, that we are all enslaved, that we are all in need of the liberating Gospel.

The commissioners? The commissioners are also victims. Like Orwell's imperialists, they are trapped by the very system they have created. Imagining themselves powerful men immune to the influence of the public, they must act like powerful men immune to the influence of the public. They must act out their scenario of aggression without consideration of the cost to themselves or to others. Claiming no alternatives can exist, they are slaves to their own imaginations, victims of the inevitable violence of their own willfulness. They are more to be pitied than hated.

March 29

From the *World Book* my parents bought when I was in elementary school, I learned that our word *Lent* comes from the old English word, *lenten,* which means "spring." It hardly seems up to bearing the burden of meaning it has come to have. It seems so pagan.

Sitting here this morning with nothing much on my mind such paganness seems okay. These woods are far from "church." Far from the muttered words that tame the wildness of God. Here I sit on the edge between the domestic and the wild. Along the fence line I've piled brush. Birds inhabit it and pass berry seeds. Brambles grow up. More birds come to them. Rabbits hide in the cover. In the summer, deer bed down in it to escape the midday heat.

I walk along the edge of the brambles choosing to stay near, but choosing not to invade or destroy them for they are my access to lives not mine. And those lives are an access to the life of the Creator.

He is here revealing Himself as surely as He reveals Himself in words. But as I cannot seize the lives of the creatures, I cannot seize the life of the

Creator. I must wait and let it occur about me and in me. Wordlessly. Silently.

And it is good.

I am filled. Sunlight spills across the floor.

March 30

At the old Royal again. A cold, rainy morning, not yet 8:00 A.M. I'm writing early because Melissa has an eye infection and I must drive her to the ophthalmologist in Olean. No woods today.

After two weeks of quiet in which I was able to meditate and think on some of the spiritual dimensions and discipline involved in the dump resistance, I am being turned back to activity. The commission has announced that they will try to gain access to the Caneadea site next Thursday—April 5. The expectation is that the confrontation will take place at my corner.

My schedule for the week looks like this:

Sunday:　　　Opening day of trout season—we will serve chili and coffee and hand out information to fishermen at Allen Lake, a popular trout pond near the Caneadea site.

Monday: Several of us will be guests at the
             Rotary Club when Rochester Gas and
             Electric Company makes its presenta-
             tion favoring nuclear energy.

Tuesday: Final planning session for action

Thursday: Confrontation

Besides that, I have, of course, my classes and
regular activities at home and at church. Monday
morning I have an appointment with my cardiolo-
gist—in all this I need a heart doctor, not one to
listen to my pump, one to administer to my anxiety
and fear.

After getting into a discussion last week in
which numbers (half-lives and rads) began to figure,
I vowed never to let that happen again. Of the
generating of numbers there is no end. And the
question, "How much radiation is safe?" is like the
old joke, "Can I do it 'till I need glasses?" Earth
abuse is self-abuse, and we live in a culture that is
more than half blind. Only the fact that we wear
contacts lets us pretend that all is well.

I've been reading Thomas Merton's *Alaskan
Conferences.* In one of them he tells a wonderful story
of two old hermits who decide that to be normal they
should have a fight.

One says, "Fine, what can we fight over?"

The other says, "We need to own something.

People fight over things." So he goes out, gets a brick, and puts it between them. Then he says, "That's mine!"

The first responds, "Fine. You can have it."

Unable to want anything, he is unable to fight.

In a later lecture Merton goes back to this story: "You can extend that to any limits you like—wherever things have become more important than people, we are in trouble. That is the crux of the whole matter." Merton extends it to war and writes about Vietnam.

I would extend the story to apply to the dump. The thing being fought over is not Chuck Barnes's farm. The things being fought over are air conditioners in the northeast, self-defrosting refrigerators, twenty-four-hour coffee pots, and other extravagant "necessities." We want to be always comfortable— 72 degrees winter and summer. We want never to handle ice, unless it's to cool our drinks. We want our morning coffee in two minutes, not ten. And for that we're willing to rape and pillage.

"How much radiation will we accept in trade for things?" My answer is simple. When the economy is done with a piece of land, how long will it be before I can grow a garden on it? If the answer requires me to wait longer than next spring, the land has been sinned against. The terms of stewardship have been violated. Our task is to tend the garden.

March 31

I cut and split the ash I dropped last week. I now have two of my eight face cords of wood in for next winter. Though it tires me, and gives me stiff muscles because I work sporadically, the direct simplicity of working in the woods is always restorative. It always ends in joy.

I'm sitting in my office now looking across the quad to the chapel. Behind me on my desk, I have a stack of papers to grade. I've read through them, and I know that they aren't bad, yet I haven't been able to force myself to get at them. The necessity of passing judgment depresses me. It seems so alien to teaching, to offering to a student what little wisdom and insight I've learned. Too little thought is given to wisdom in the education industry. Dead End. So be it.

Yesterday at the ophthalmologist office, as I waited for Melissa, I finished Merton's *Alaska Conferences.* I was filled with ideas I wanted to write about, insights into my concerns about the dump, but today, as the move from contemplation to action draws near, my mind is a blank. It is as if I've gone into some kind of shock. Feelings have ceased. All internal mechanisms have shut down. I'm locked into the course of action that has been set, and all I can do is hope—I cannot even pray—that my heart was right, my motives as pure as possible, when I made my commitment.

Is action, perhaps, a kind of silence? Or is it a

shout? Perhaps it is neither; perhaps it is simply a yielding.

One thought, however, does surface, a fear. Several Sundays ago, when I spoke to the gathering about non-violence, I said the end of non-violence was not victory. I said the end was the winning of the other to your side. I said non-violence was not opposition, but a kind of wooing. During the question period someone asked me if I really believed that our action could convert the siting commission. I flubbed my answer. I was afraid to say yes. I was afraid that saying yes would be going too far, that if I said yes the questioner would laugh. So I said, "Ideally that is the object, but I think we have to be realistic as well. Those we can convert are those who are unsure. The siting commission is probably lost."

That moment keeps returning to me. It's easy to see now what I should have said. But what I fear is that my answer reveals my lack of faith, reveals that I do not yet believe what I affirm. And if I do not believe, can I know how I will act in the crisis?

Merton comments that "Non-violence has become all fouled up and is turning into a kind of semi-violence." I see that around me. Hanging the governor in effigy is violence. Stuffing a road kill skunk into the ventilation system of the commission's van is violence. Leaving carcasses in the commission's office in Cortland County is violence. Hating the commissioners is violence.

Fifth Sunday in Lent
April Fools' Day
Passion Sunday
Opening of Trout Season
Daylight Savings Time

With a heading like that, how should I begin? Some random thoughts.

The exercise of power over nature is possible. In the short term we are strong. We can alter the face of the earth. The exercise of power, however, is, without exception, destructive to the possibility of living in relationship—in mutuality—with nature. Power is founded on opposition—one will against and prevailing over another. Exercising power over people has the same results; relationship is destroyed. Winning is losing. Always.

Our existing economic-social structures are built on the exercising of power. Even ACNAG operates this way. Such structures are intrinsically evil. By participating in them (and I/we can never do otherwise) we compromise ourselves. The best we can do is manage an accommodation with the structures that provide for the promise of healing in our broken relationships. This is both the bondage to sin St. Paul addresses and the hope of the resurrection.

A couple of weeks ago, when the siting commission sent its "information van" around the county, I struggled with how to respond. Some chose to demonstrate and passed out counter-information. Some carried signs, others blocked parking spaces so the van could not stop. On the last day of its visits, another group engaged it directly. They poured buck scent on its carpet. They stuffed a dead skunk into its ventilation system. And they hung an effigy of the governor from its bumper. Then they marched it out of town—a modern version of a tar-and-feathering. Though their action actually hurt no one, it was violent. It had no redemptive qualities, no possibility of winning over.

On the day the van came to Fillmore I thought I would try something different. I determined to wear my orange armband, buy coffee and donuts, and enter the van. I planned to say something like, "You come here intending to do violence to a land and people that I love. I intend to stand in your way, but I also intend you to know that I do not oppose you. I oppose only your action, and I invite you to see the violence of what you are engaged in and to join us in refusing to continue it." I didn't do it. I got to the scene and found nearly a hundred protesters had forced the van out of town. I could just see it parked near the bridge over the river; the long walk to it in defiance of protesters was too much for me. I rationalized my way out of going. I argued, "There's no one in the van to influence. If I go, I'll be counted as a 'visit' and be turned into a siting commission number to be used against me." Both arguments were true. But they shouldn't have mattered. The men in the van were not decision makers, but they were human beings caught up in the same tragic/comic mess as the rest of us. And I should not have been worrying about becoming a number when no one trusts the numbers anyway. In short, I chickened out. I played Peter at the trial, and the cock has been crowing ever since.

These are all good thoughts for April Fools' Day and Passion Sunday. Another fool has crucified Christ.

And now my heater has quit. I'm out of propane.

In the sermon this morning one sentence stood out to me: "We never become too old or too holy to need to die." We need to die all the day long. Our lives need to become holy deaths. I think that is one of the things I've been learning, not only by sitting here day after day setting down these reflections, but by working in these woods. In both actions I am engaged in a slow uncovering of a self defined by an unfolding relationship that can be summed up in the brief sentence, "I am my brother's keeper." I am my brother's keeper, not in the sense of keeping him behind bars, but in the sense of keeping him well (on his terms, not mine) for the sake of the Lord. Who is my brother? My brother is Christ in all things. I keep Him for the day of His return.

What I must do here in my woods is learn what was being made here before the willful intrusion of sin, what will be made given time and non-interference. Then I must work within the limit of my knowledge—acknowledging that I work in ignorance—to allow that work of grace being done apart from and through me to come to completion. I am part of it all—the sin and the grace. Only as I die to myself, all the day long, can I be a part of the grace.

April 2

We met last night to go over the plans for Thursday. We made the final decisions about the locations of roadblocks. And we confirmed the decision to wear masks, plain yellow orbs with mushrooms on them to remind the walkover team of their mushroom joke: "Protest leaders keep the citizens in the dark and feed them horse manure." The masks will keep the police from making identifications during the day and serving injunctions on people at a later date. To serve injunctions they will have to take the time to make arrests.

Now everything is focused. All my thoughts connect. Before going to bed I read in Thomas Merton, "We are prisoners of a process, a dialectic of false promises and real deceptions leading to futility." It is that process we wish to break, that process of selling our *selves* for things.

Then the nightmares returned. I had three. I woke from the first screaming, from the second crying, and from the third with no clear memory, with only that vague unsettledness that comes from having dreamed unpleasantly.

In the first dream I went into a bookstore. The books were there, but when I picked them up they were empty. They had all been made into movies. I held one before me and stared at the blank pages. Suddenly I was being sucked into it through the pages into a blackness, into a kind of wind tunnel. Terror overwhelmed me and I screamed.

The second was more vague. I was at home. For some reason I had all the artwork in the house stacked on the bed. I think I was on my knees leaning against the frames to keep them from sliding to the floor. The frames cut my face. Linda kept calling me from another room. Something was wrong between us. I could not go to her without toppling the art, and for a reason I do not know she could only call me. I woke sobbing.

The third I've lost. Perhaps mercifully. The first two are clear enough. That I dreamed them the night of Passion Sunday is not lost. I've little taste for crucifixion. Mine or anyone else's.

April 3

For the first time my students are suffering from my involvement with the dump resistance. My classes are fine (I think). When I'm actually teaching, my engagement with the students and the subject takes over, but the minute I leave class, the plans for Thursday return. Thoughts of all that might happen

run wild in my imagination, and I am useless. I can't
force myself to sit before a set of papers and work.
Even when I know the papers are good and will
require only small comments, the discipline is beyond my reach. I am nervous and afraid.

April 4

From this morning's Psalms:

The Lord will give strength unto his people; the
Lord will bless his people with peace. (29:11)

I will extol thee, O Lord for thou hast lifted me
up, and hast not made my foes to rejoice over
me. O Lord, my God, I cried unto thee, and
thou hast healed me. (30:1–2)

In thee, O Lord, do I put my trust; let me never
be ashamed; deliver me speedily: be thou my
strong rock, for an house of defense to save me.
For thou art my rock and my fortress; therefore
for thy name's sake lead me and guide me. Pull
me out of the net that they have laid privily for
me: for thou art my strength. Into thine hand I
commit my spirit: thou hast redeemed me, O
Lord God of truth.

    Have mercy upon me, O Lord, for I am in
trouble: mine eye is consumed with grief, yea,
my soul and my belly.

    My times are in thy hand: deliver me from
the hand of mine enemies and from them that
persecute me.

O love the Lord; all his saints: for the Lord
preserveth the faithful, and plentifully rewar-
deth the proud doer. Be of good cheer, and he
shall strengthen your heart, all ye that hope in
the Lord. (31:1–5, 9, 15, 23–24)

I recognize that these verses are not promises.
Reading them this morning does not mean that
tomorrow I will not be arrested. Neither does
reading them this morning mean that tomorrow the
people of Allegany County will prevail. The Lord's
ways are mysterious, and my will is often not His
will. At best I sometimes will His will. That is what
I'm trying to do now. The thing I take from these
psalms is the assurance that He is my strength and
that all I have to offer is my faithfulness, my willing
myself into His hands. I do that. And so, while I fear
for the moment, I do not fear for His purposes or my
part in them.

Before coming here this morning, I had breakfast at the home of my division chair with three other
faculty and three students being honored at chapel
today for their academic achievement. It was a huge
breakfast and a pleasant time. Christ was there with
us as we rejoiced together, and I went away encouraged that He indeed will continue to raise up His
people.

From breakfast I drove to Caneadea where I met
the Bogeyman, the coordinator for tomorrow's action. We walked the bridge where we anticipate
encountering the siting team, tested our radios, and
made our last-minute decisions.

I've picked up the chain saw and come-along (a hand winch) and have them in the car. We hope there is no need for the chain saw, but some have threatened to drop trees behind the police to block them in. Surrounding them is the one action we have been told will precipitate force on their part. We want to be ready to clear the way for them should that happen. I've also loaded two sleeping bags into the car should we have to deal with hypothermia.

As I look at the planned action and my part in it, I wonder at how it has come to be. Quiet, non-confrontational me, the fool on the hill, the poet in the woods, lining up to face down the state police, the marshalled forces of the State of New York. Just saying no. I think I have come to this by obedience. And I think this obedience will change my life once more. Having come to this point of commitment, how can I retreat without giving up the truths I have embraced? I cannot. The earth is the Lord's. Standing for it, I stand for its Creator and proclaim Christ has come to redeem His own.

Tomorrow's action, however it ends, will be a beginning. I read, yesterday, an interview with the Zen poet Lucian Stryk. He said,

> One can not have, in Zen, two masters: one that guides and challenges the disciple to revolutionize his or her spirit, and another political or ideological one. But the full commitment to spiritual practice by no means precludes an involvement with social concerns. There is no solipsism in Zen. To the contrary,

Zen practice may be seen as a ripening of the subject for a more profound and effective engagement with the world. In fact, this is the disciple's vow, to act compassionately for others. . . .

What is important to recognize is that in the Buddhist world view, there can be no meaningful social change without an equally radical transformation of spirit.

What he says of Zen is true also of life in Christ. I have one master, and He is not the economy, nor is He my greed (though both have mastered me). He is the Christ, and what I have—possessions and talent—is His. Now and forever.

Snow has fallen this morning. When I got up at 6:30, it lay lightly on the lawn, the green showing through. It has continued now for five hours, and the woods are made new with its soft beauty. Outside the cabin the hemlock, heavy with its burden hangs low over the door. The dark green of the needles an undertone to the whiteness. Nothing has been moving since the snowfall began, the only tracks are mine. And as I sit here, the only sound disturbing the silence is the soft thump of snow landing on the roof after slipping from overloaded hemlock branches. I am ready and I am at peace.

My times, O Lord, are in thy hands.

April 5

Today is the day. The siting commission will seek to gain access to the Caneadea site. All our plans are in place, and in a few minutes I will be leaving for my station at the bridge. I woke at 3:00 A.M. from a nightmare. In it the police had somehow circled around our barrier and were behind us. Aggressively, without making distinctions or reading the injunction, they began to arrest spectators. I had to get up, make toast, and drink a glass of orange juice to shake the oppressiveness of the dream, to compose myself so I could sleep again.

April 6

The morning began as we planned. I went to the bridge at 7:30, met the other monitors and the six grandparents who had volunteered to be the first arrestees. Cars streamed past us heading for the gathering spot at the German Settlement Church on the site. The numbers encouraged us. At 9:00 we put on our masks. Two resisters locked a chain to one side of the bridge and placed plywood on the open deck so chairs could be set up. Another climbed into the steelwork of the bridge and tied a large flag directly overhead. Others moved farm equipment to the end of the bridge: a disk, a large tractor, and a wood wagon.

When word reached us by radio that the siting team was about five miles away, the chain was pulled across the bridge and locked. The grandparents moved forward, took their chairs, and handcuffed themselves to the chain. Behind them resisters unfurled a large banner, "GRANDPARENTS FOR THE FUTURE." The bridge was closed with the farm equipment, and about a hundred demonstrators moved into place.

When Sheriff Scholes arrived with the "walkover" team and state troopers, he greeted the grandparents. After a few moments of conversation, he retreated to discuss the situation with the troopers. He returned, had the injunction read, and when the grandparents refused to move, called the troopers to remove them. When they arrived, Alexandra Landis, an eighty-seven-year-old Harvard Ph.D., unwrapped a carefully folded flag and made a brief speech asking that it be returned to President Bush. We learned later the flag had adorned the coffin of her son, a veteran of World War II.

Then the arrests began. As they proceeded, the resisters staged a slow march up the hill toward the next roadblock. I retreated with them about a quarter of a mile to a vantage point from which I could watch the bridge. When it was cleared, and the troopers started over it about an hour later, I radioed ahead and raced up the hill. The moment I reached the waiting group of protesters, a five-bottom plow was backed across the road and dropped. When I got out of my car, I met Melissa, my daughter. She had been serving food three miles away, but curiosity had overcome her. We stood and talked, waiting for what would come.

Within minutes, the sheriff, the "walk-over" team, and the troopers approached the blockade. Once more a deputy read the injunction. Then everything changed. The troopers formed a phalanx (there were about forty of them), moved around the barrier, and marched into the crowd, scattering it as it tried to move backward in an orderly fashion. In this confusion Melissa and I were separated.

The troopers moved aggressively forward. Since I was on the radio, and could not afford to risk arrest so early in the action, I hiked through six-inch snow in the fields along the road. I could not keep up with the front of the line, so I deliberately dropped back to keep track of the arrests being made and relayed that forward to the base radio.

The troopers arrested at random. They took retreating protesters from behind, and they took spectators from the side of the road. They made no distinctions between people blocking the road and people watching. It was my nightmare being worked out in the waking world.

As the phalanx moved ahead, the distance the troopers had to walk arrestees increased. They made fewer arrests. But some of them were dramatic; they arrested the co-chairman of the Concerned Citizens of Allegany County. She was standing beside the road, unmasked, playing her guitar and singing. Everyone in the county knows that she has refused to participate in civil disobedience because the CCAC is committed to working in the courts. When she protested she was not breaking any law, she was told, "We have to stop your singing." The troopers' intent seemed to be to disrupt the organization of the protest and to create as much uncertainty as they could. Nothing in their actions seemed to be directed toward calming anxiety or stabilizing the situation. With my radio I stood off to the side, observing like a dispassionate writer, narrating what I saw for those ahead of me. Only today in my exhaustion, do I realize just how passionately I was involved.

While I narrated, I also listened to another monitor narrating. "Minnow" was with the phalanx. (I learned later, when I caught up, that Melissa was also with the phalanx. She was staying out of reach of it, but she was staying with it, "Jumping ditches," she said, "I didn't know I could jump!" She also described the retreat as a flight, a wild run to stay ahead of the advancing troopers.)

As I approached a crest I could not see over, Minnow came on the radio, "A group of riders on horses are coming," he said. "They're approaching the troopers. They've stopped. The troopers have stopped. The troopers are trying to push them back. The horses are backing. Now they're turning around. The troopers are among them. A trooper is trying to grab a horse."

The action coordinator interrupted, "They're grabbing the horses?"

"Yes. The trooper's caught hold of one. He has his nightstick out."

"They've drawn nightsticks?" the coordinator asked.

A wave of sickness hit me. *Oh God!* I thought, *Not this. Where's Melissa! Please don't let her be there.*

"Yes," Minnow answered. "They're hitting the horses. They're hitting the rider."

The coordinator interrupted again, "Hitting the horses? Hitting the riders?"

"Yes. They've got one of the riders. They're trying to drag him from the horse. They have him pulled off and they're beating on him. They have him on the ground."

About that time I came over the crest and could see the action ahead of me. Most of the troopers were still in a block. Ahead of them, the horses were still or circling slowly. Then two troopers led a demonstrator past me. He seemed to be holding his hand, and one of the troopers was asking him about it. A horse and rider approached them and side-stepped a few paces away. The troopers threatened the rider, who hassled them verbally and then retreated.

As I scanned the group of demonstrators, which was fragmented, stunned, and largely silent, I saw Melissa off to one side, standing in the woods. She was not alone. I went up to her and touched her gently on the shoulder. She turned, and I held her. "You've come at just the right time," she said. "I can't believe what I just saw." The person with her greeted me and raised her mask. A friend. Her husband was missing, and she wanted to know if he'd been arrested. He had.

We stood together watching the dwindling group of protesters mill about the troopers. Then the troopers gathered, turned, and began a slow march back down the road. The demonstrators surged to the middle of the road, cheered, and followed them a short ways before allowing them to proceed alone. The confrontation was over.

Palm Sunday

Though three days have passed since the demonstration, neither Linda nor I has calmed down. Yesterday, to escape we went to Olean to see *Driving Miss Daisy*. It did not help. On the way the tension was so great we could not talk. Linda's need for surety, for security and safety, directly conflicts with my increasing need, as the rhetoric escalates, to risk more, to refuse to be intimidated. Both needs are real and understandable. I think both exist in each of us. I know I'd like to run away, to say it's too much for me, and let what happens happen. But the drive forward to validate what has already been done is a force as strong as—rather stronger—than the fear.

That drive, in fact, has been behind me since writing *In Season and Out*. My commitment was shaped that long ago.

This morning two things rage in me: my hatred of the nuclear industry as a totalitarian institution, and my inability to feel any sustained anger at the police. Since at least 1977 when I chose to begin heating with wood and made deliberate efforts to shape my life within the limits of good stewardship, I have objected to the nuclear industry on two grounds. First, it abuses the earth; it destroys. And second, it concentrates power in the hands of a few technocrats who then determine the fate of both the earth and the creatures of the earth. This concentration is evident in the attitude the siting commission has taken toward the people of Allegany County. From the beginning they have assured us that we are incompetent to make our own decisions, that we haven't the information necessary. Every time someone disagrees, no matter what his qualifications, the siting commission simply says, "He hasn't educated himself. He is speaking from understandable, but unnecessary fears. Trust us, we know the truth." All disagreement is attributed to ignorance.

A particular example of this is the commission chairman's condescending remarks about the grandparents on the bridge. Without seeking to learn anything about them, he called them the dupes of cynical, exploitative leaders. It is clear he doesn't try to understand. He speaks the world as he wishes it to be. It is also clear he doesn't know the undupable senior citizens I know.

The victims in this are not the grandparents; the victims are the state troopers called upon to execute the orders of the institutions of power. When men are dressed in uniforms, lined in ranks, and marched in formation, they lose (and this is the point of it all) their identity. They become a part of an abstract force. The tragedy is that they do not lose their human fears, and when they meet what they perceive to be a threat, they react both as humans and as an abstract force; they strike out against what frightens them. When the police officer grabbed the horse, he was not thinking; he was reacting as any frightened human might react. I cannot blame him (though he did not use good judgment). In his place I might have done the same. The fault lies with the one who ordered him into that situation. But even he was ordered. Behind him were the totalitarian impulses of the power industry and the state.

* * *

I write this on a day given to remembering the triumphant entry of Christ into Jerusalem. This year the day seems empty. The events of the week are too overpowering. The knowledge that Christ's entry led directly to His crucifixion looms too dark ahead. This seems the strangest holiday of the year, a celebration of a misunderstanding. Those who shouted "Hosanna" to Christ expected some kind of worldly kingship from Him. In this world, though our hearts long for it and our lives incline toward it, the kingdom has not yet come.

April 9

Holy Week begins and I near the end of this journal. I am glad for both. For forty-one days now I've been beating out words, thinking, thinking, thinking about my every action, and I am tired. I wonder what good all these words have done. I know nothing now that I did not know at the beginning—except, perhaps, the deviousness of my own mind and heart. I set out to explore the meaning of the redemption of creation, but I've explored only my wandering thoughts, my errant emotions: anger, sorrow, occasional joy. I've come to think that the meaning of the redemption of creation cannot be explored in words; it must rather be worked out in living relationships. In tending to stewardship responsibilities, in living in Christ, we live in the process of the redemption. Living within it, we cannot comment objectively for the redemption of creation is an idea larger even than personal salvation. Personal salvation is just one small part of it.

So what do I know? Mostly my brokenness, my inability to maintain a non-violent (to say nothing of a loving) stance toward those Christ calls me to love, my need for the coming of grace, which this week marks. I want to stand beside Christ Triumphant riding into Jerusalem, turning over the tables of the moneychangers, turning over the injustices of the world, setting up a kingdom now. I want a victory. It's as simple as that.

Peter, when Christ revealed His coming sufferings, said, "Lord, this shall not be unto thee." We all know how Christ replied. How many times I have said in this journal, in my desire to have my will worked, "Lord this shall not be unto thee." How often I have played Peter.

The earth is the Lord's. He has chosen to risk it by giving it over to the stewardship of humans. No matter how I try, I shall never be more than a bumbling gardener. By what right do I rage at others who do no better? By what right do I rage at those who do worse? And how, lost in the overwhelming task, do I tell who does better and who does worse?

The events of last Thursday, and my inability to put them behind me, weigh on me. I wonder if I'm not beginning to question how I entered into them. I intended to do right. I intended to be faithful. Can anyone do more than that? What good can come of second guessing? Humility?

Had I the day to do over, given the knowledge I had, I would do it again. Going forward with the knowledge I now have, both about the willingness of the institutions of power to use violence, and my own responses, I can only pray that at the next moment of decision I will have grace and wisdom, for at that moment my present knowledge will be as insufficient as my past knowledge was. I must act in hope and faith. Knowledge, like last year's words, is never sufficient for this year's test.

I understand what has been troubling me. Several days back I quoted Thomas Merton on the subtle intrusion of a kind of semi-violence into a non-violent commitment. Thursday a slight shift took place in our action. We introduced semi-violence. We used a kind of force and threat. First, for what appeared to be good reasons, we hid behind masks. They were designed to be non-threatening. Yet here is what one reporter, a friend of ACNAG wrote: "I knew I was among friends . . . but in that early morning gloom I felt very uneasy surrounded by yellow masks concealing the smiling urgent faces I've gotten to know so well over the year.

"I can't quite explain it, but the feeling haunted me all day, whenever I looked at those expressionless, passionless, yellow orbs." If she felt that, I wonder what the state troopers, men from out of town who took no pleasure in their job, must have felt facing us. Did we create the fear that drove them so relentlessly forward?

Second, for what also appeared to be a good reason, the need to halt that advancing wedge of gray, we used horses. We cannot pretend that in using them we were not meeting force with force. We did not intend actual violence, but no longer trusting the moral authority of our offered bodies, and not willing to accept the possibility of the temporary triumph of evil, we met evil with evil.

We cannot allow that to happen. It will do us no good to save the world at the price of our souls.

We cannot be ruled by our fear of crucifixion. We came down off our cross to nail the pharisees.

April 11

Outside, a spattering of half-snow/half-rain coats the trees and ground. The temperature is about 33 or 34 and it is falling. I have a full cup of coffee, a fresh donut, and no propane. I thought I had about an hour's worth, but it's no go. I turned on the heater, watched it turn red, and then slowly fade to nothing. I will write in the cold until my hands freeze and my coffee is gone.

It is difficult to turn my thoughts to meditations on Holy Week with so much still happening. Last night I watched the videos from Thursday's action and then talked with the other monitors until 11:00 about what we saw and what we should consider for the future. Though there is no division within the group, we are pushing different directions in our thinking; we have different personalities and different kinds of commitments. Some are more political in their orientation; they stress the importance of winning in maintaining our popular support. They do not want to be doormats. Though they remain committed to avoiding overt violence, they are willing to consider intimidation as a tactic. And they want to stay out of the courts, which they do not trust.

Others of us are more strongly oriented to the moral dimension of non-violence. I spoke of Merton's caution about the introduction of semi-violence into the protest, and I voiced my sense that we, not the police, are the ones ultimately responsible for the tone. The police by definition are given to meeting violence with violence—controlled and reasonable violence, but violence. That's why they carry sticks and wear automatics on their hips. A truly non-violent action would give them no excuse to escalate an encounter.

All agreed with me in theory. Some agreed in practice and wish, as I do, to engage the police and siting commission with nothing but our presence and the moral authority of our convictions. Others recognized the difficulty of that stance. It means giving the state as many arrestees as the state wants. It means submitting people of limited resources to exorbitant fines imposed by a judge whose rulings in favor of the siting commission in the past have been questionable. Their concern for the welfare of the people facing that power is not a side issue. It is one of the complicating factors that we must deal with. It is part of the bondage of sin that forces us to make, not absolute decisions, but the best compromises possible.

As I ponder this, I think that perhaps this struggle is more appropriate to Holy Week than I first thought. I keep returning to the crowd that cheered Christ's triumphant ride into Jerusalem. What were they thinking? If they had not seen Him raise Lazarus, they had heard about it. They knew He was coming in power, and they expected a king who would free them from Roman oppression. (I tell you, when I watched those troopers march into the crowd, I thought of the Roman army.) We cannot dismiss their expectations and criticize their lack of spiritual discernment. Christ fooled everyone. Dare I suggest that if He did not fool Himself, He at least had moments where He considered the popular scenario? I doubt if liberation theology is unique to the twentieth century. And I wonder what that crowd thought when He reached Jerusalem and began to go about His business. In that week He cast out the money changers, and when challenged by the chief priests and scribes, He silenced them with conundrums. His followers must have believed something great was about to happen. Surely He was going to rally them. Surely He was going to lead them against the oppression. After all, the Jewish story is the story of the Exodus, the story of political liberation. It is only Christians, looking backward, who focus on the Creation/Fall story, that see redemption and restoration—forgiveness of sins— as the central story of God's dealing with humans.

What do I make of this week of conflicting

implications of those stories? What do I say, after a month of praying the psalms with their talk, their unending talk of enemies and victories over enemies? Why should I not be thinking of victory over oppressors? Why should I be thinking of giving myself up to be crucified?

Is crucifixion required? I remember writing in a notebook, "Everyone wants to be Christlike, but no one wants to be crucified." The implication of that remark is that every Christian must be crucified. But if we are Christ's body, His incarnation in the world, isn't His historical crucifixion enough? Or does His crucifixion continue in the crucifixion, persecution, of His saints in the world?

I simply do not know. I do not understand.

I return to obedience. I must be obedient to my call to be a steward. I find where that takes me as I go forward, carried both by intention and circumstance. My hope remains in Christ, in grace, and it is lost in mystery.

Maundy Thursday

The students have left for Easter break, and the college is closed, so I am off schedule. Though it is still bitter cold—snow has been swirling off and on all day—the afternoon sun brightens my cabin and warms the atmosphere, if not the temperature. I am comfortable thanks to my last tank of propane. When this one is finished, I will declare the season changed and call every day warm.

On the way up I had to stop for a woodchuck. I saw him ahead of me, a small brown lump on the tire tracks in the road. I slowed and when he did not move, wondered if he'd been hit by someone else. As I approached, I steered to go around him. Suddenly he raised his head, then ambled slowly into my path. But I was down to second gear and barely moving. I waited for him to reach the side of the road and pulled up beside him. He waddled, his fat derriere shaking like a comic tutu, through the ditch and up the bank into the woodlot. I rolled down the window to speak to him; I wanted to instruct him, to give him some advice about automobiles and idiot drivers who charge 50 mph up this dirt road, but he had no mind to listen. I wished him a good day anyway and turned into the woods.

Now I sit adjusting my mind, listening to the wind, a low moaning about the cabin, and the cawing of a crow—crows. Too curious to sit still, I went out to see them. They occupied the tops of the hemlocks directly over the cabin. When I moved around the corner, a dark silent shadow dropped through the trees and glided off. Too many branches shielded it from my view, so I had only a glimpse of it. Perhaps an owl? That would make sense. The crows continued to scold, directing their attention to me, then, still yakking, flapped off to the other side of the gully and settled in the distant woods. In the time it has taken to write this they have grown quiet, and I am once more alone.

But I am not alone. I bring with me to this place the presences of others. Today I bring with me those I sat with at the noon communion service, those friends I have worshiped with so many years, those friends from whom I take the comfort of the presence of Christ, those friends in whose presence I feel I am home. Linda and I sat in nearly the last occupied row. Only Bud and Carol were behind us, and when Bud began to sing and I recognized his voice, I felt a peace descend on me.

I looked ahead and saw Gus Prinsell, our physician for twenty-five years. And I remember the time he came to us in the middle of the night during a snowstorm in the days we waited for Linda to have her heart surgery. He prayed with us, and more than medicine, he brought us Christ. I thought what a privilege it has been to live a witness to the life of this good man.

From him I looked across the church to Aileen Shea, artist and retired pastor's wife. And I thought of her letter just this week to the college newspaper in response to a column written by a student doubter. She did not judge. Instead she told how within the last year, as a result of external circumstances and the challenges of a friend, she too had endured a time of questioning and fear. She told how having endured it, she knew a greater peace than before, and she reached out encouraging, understanding, and making it okay to be young and full of questions.

Near her I saw Gordon Stockin, erudite, gentle Emeritus Professor of Greek and Latin. Though it would make him blush to read these words, a man as Christlike as any I have known. Without his kindness to me when I was a student, I would not be here. And now he endures his own testing, the wild growth of cancer, a raging within him contrary to his spirit, contrary to the life of Christ indwelling him, and he bears it graciously.

With these and others I went to the altar. I broke from the loaf held out for me a crust and dipped it in the wine. I ate the body and blood of Christ. And I returned to my seat, my eyes filled with tears, my spirit filled with joy, with a sense of Christ present in the room, with a sense of belonging, with the knowledge of my membership in His body burning in my throat.

And then I came here. To be alone. But not alone. Never alone. For the union transcends the short distances I have placed between myself and them.

This morning I read in preparation for a new course I'm teaching next fall. (If only students knew how far ahead we work!) In her essay "Heart in Hiding," Katherine Paterson writes,

> I don't think morality is the basic theme of the Bible. I think its theme is closer to what physicists would call beauty. By itself, morality

is not beautiful enough. Listen to Genesis:
"And God said, Let there be light: and there
was light. And God saw the light, that it was
good: . . . And God saw everything that he had
made, and behold, it was very good." The
word "good" is not a moral judgment, but an
aesthetic one. God saw that what he had made
was very beautiful. . . .

But the Bible says something more: that
the posture of the eternal Creator toward the
finite creation is that of good will. Listen . . . to
Gerard Manley Hopkins:

The world is charged with the grandeur of
God.

It will flame out, like shining from shook
foil;

It gathers to a greatness, like the ooze of
oil

Crushed . . .

As I sit here the world *is charged* with the
grandeur of God—the saints at Houghton Church,
the woodchuck, the crow, and the owl. It is by that
grandeur that I know my unworthiness. And it is by
that grandeur that I come to grace, for that grandeur
is grace. It is the presence of Christ in this world
moving to restore the wholeness of that morning
when God said that it was good.

It is this vision that enlivens hope in me. It is
this vision that makes me a servant of all that is.

What will come of our efforts to halt the siting of
a dump in this valley, I do not know. I do not need to
know. How long I will be a part of ACNAG, I do not

know. But this I do know: Christ is in the world redeeming the world, and by His grace I am part of His body, now and forever.

Good Friday

I ended yesterday's journal entry so positively. Then for no reason, as I drove down the hill into the valley—perhaps a news item on the radio stirred my memory, I don't know. I don't know if it was even news time—the memory of an unspeakable crime I'd heard narrated on a television talk show woke in me, and my imagination went wild.

Is crucifixion required? I don't know, but it is a fact. What kind of God do I affirm?

April 14

I think this will be the last entry in this journal. How can I end a journey through Lent on Saturday? How can I stop when Christ lies in the tomb? All that is literary in me, all that believes and wants to testify to the resurrection wants to go on. Yet, the action of this journal, the movement in time toward a resolution of the one issue dominating the thought of this county, is in suspension. The siting commission has not withdrawn. Their spokeswoman made very clear yesterday that they do not intend to withdraw.

Speaking to reporters she reminded them that Governor Cuomo has not suspended the job of the task force; he has only asked that they not return in the "recent future." I'm not sure what the recent future is, but I strongly suspect that it is similar to the recent past, and I am not anxious for it to arrive.

Moving forward to Easter requires an affirmation that I am unable to make, for completing the action of the journal with the Resurrection implies on my part a confidence that the uncompleted action of this piece will end the same way. I have no such faith. And I refuse to manufacture such a faith.

Christ rules. Of that I have no doubt. But what He might allow to come to pass, I fear. He makes us no promises about the conditions under which we will live in this world. Where does that leave me on this gray afternoon beneath the hemlocks?

*   *   *

Yesterday in my reading I came across a story about Desmond Tutu. He reportedly said something about God being present in events, but not nearly obviously enough to satisfy his need to see Him clearly. I read the passage to Linda, and said, "That's the way I feel."

She answered, "You aren't paying attention."

Perhaps I'm not paying attention. Perhaps I haven't eyes to see. I once received a letter from one of my readers telling me she was praying for me to meet the Lord because I sounded as if I really wanted to know Him. What can I say?

Because I'm writing this, I went to church yesterday afternoon—the community Good Friday service I usually skip. I went dressed for the woods because I'd arranged to meet Jim Wolfe, an ecologist friend, to do some work afterward. The service began at 1:30. Nothing about it pleased me. Now I know that doesn't matter. I long ago gave up going to church to be pleased. I go to identify myself with the body of Christ present in the gathering, and I can usually set aside any aggravations resulting from worship style or aggressive theologizing. But yesterday I was helpless. Even the voices of the participating ministers grated on me. One reminded me of Truman Capote. Another sounded as if he were speaking around a mouthful of marbles. And a third came down on alternate words as if he were trying to split them with an ax. Thwack. Thwack. Meanings flew everywhere.

At 2:30 I looked at my order of service. Four more preachers, two hymns, a solo, the offering, and several prayers to go. I slipped out the back. They could get through the rest without me. I met Jim and headed for the woods.

We drove up to Pike, turned up Telegraph Hill, and then down Alpo Road (that's not the right name, but that's what has stuck in my head). We pulled off onto a dirt road leading to a Free Methodist camp along Wiscoy Creek. I'd never been there and was startled to find a lovely small lake less than a mile from the main road we'd left in Pike. We took a canoe and paddled to the inlet where Jim took a water sample. Temperature: 46 degrees, pH: 5.0. The air temperature was nearly 50 degrees, and a group of campers were splashing, fully clothed, into the lake from a water slide opposite us. I was cold. The wind blew harshly over the open water, and I wished for my gloves, but as I held the canoe steady against the wind and Jim marked his sample, I thought on the contrast of my unsettledness in the service and my calm on the water. We paddled to the middle of the lake and repeated the sampling process. I watched the water. The bottom of the lake was a maze of stumps—perfect cover for bass and panfish. I spotted clear sandy shallows where they will spawn in a few short weeks, and I suggested to Jim that his study should include a survey of the fish population, which I could help him make.

We crossed the rest of the lake to the outlet, where a Canada goose swam about ignoring us, sampled the water there, and then returned to the dock. The study Jim is doing is a result of an increased algae growth in the lake. Campers no longer want to swim in it. To combat the algae the camp owners plan to release sterile carp in the lake to eat it. The study is necessary to complete the permit process.

The plans sounded fine, but just before we left, the director asked about using copper sulfate to kill the algae. The local Agway recommended that to keep the lake clean for swimming before the carp are established. Jim was very quiet, and I sensed what was troubling him. The copper sulfate would work. It would kill the algae, but the algae would then settle to the bottom, decompose, and use up the oxygen in the water. That in turn might cause a fish kill. He said so.

Unspoken in this conversation was that hard question, the question that lies behind all stewardship issues. What's more important, the fish population or an algae-free lake for swimmers? What's more important, a harmonious living within the bounds of nature or a technological fix allowing us to do what we want now?

I tell the story because it is our story at this point in time. We face it with nuclear energy. We face it with coal-fired plants. We face it with plastics, toxins, and automobiles. "Forward to the Pleistocene," say the Earth First!–ers. While I can't quite say that, part of me would like to. What I must say is forward to a new sense of stewardship, to a greater inclusiveness in our caring.

*   *   *

I know where I am. I am here in Remnant Acres, trying my best to live responsibly, to care for the small portion of earth God has given directly to my care. It gives me great joy to be here, to do His will. If it takes me beyond this place, to the other side of the valley to stand between the siting commission and the land, I will go. If it takes me to jail, I will go.

But I hope it takes me to neither of those places. I hope it takes me right here to faith that keeps mountains in place. And I hope it takes me deeper and deeper into the community that dwells here.

As I came up Tucker Hill, about a quarter mile before my turnoff on School Farm Road, I spotted a deer, a doe feeding in the field. I stopped the car, reached into the back seat for my binoculars, and settled down to watch her. She was turned away from me, her tail a dark black stripe lined with a fringe of white flattened against her rump. I could see her head through her legs as she grazed. The legs seemed too thin to hold her weight, and they splayed out a bit as she bent, to allow her to reach the grass.

At one point she suddenly straightened. Her head came up, and then her ears, edged with black, stood tense. She glanced about, then returned to feeding. I watched her five minutes before she straightened again, looked across the field, and then bounded slowly over a rise. I waited for her to appear going up the other side, but she did not. I figured she was following the cover of the little cut to the trees, so I put the car in gear and pulled forward to look down it. Two other deer grazed with her.

Not wanting to scare them, I kept moving up the hill. I turned in on School Farm Road, and stopped the car. I took my glasses and got out. In the biting wind I stood watching them graze.

Perhaps it is because of them I can end this journal here. "One world at a time," Thoreau said as he neared death.

Thoreau was wrong. We have both worlds at once.

This world is "charged with the grandeur of God."

Five Psalms

1989–1990

I.

The clever trout that nips
the mayfly from the air
is quick to praise
the Maker of his sight.
His speckled side
reflects the light;
he swims as he
was made to swim.

The slender popple
at the meadow's edge
is in the Spirit
also giving praise.
Its lean into the wind,
its supple ways
declare it stands
as it was made to stand.

The raucous jay,
that scolding streak

of blue gives warning
to the quiet wood.
He knows my nature
is not good.
"Beware," he cries
as he was made to cry.

From these, O Lord,
the creatures of your Love's
abundance, let me learn
to forsake
the wild desire that drove
my father Adam to shake
the garden tree and claim
a glory of his own.

Before them, strike
me dumb. Let me see them
as you made them
in delight.
Then give me peace
to praise as well your bright
presence as the trout,
the popple, and the jay.

II.

When men call the earth
their own,
they turn the land
for profit;
they plow the soil
and sow their seed
in rows.

When men call the earth
their own,
they cannot be satisfied
with any crop;
they strip the soil away
and plunder riches
in the depths.

When men call the earth
their own,
they eat their souls
for food;
they soil the land
and die in wastes.

III.

Praise to you Creator Son
for all the creatures
of this earth too small
for any notice but your own.

With your eyes I see
the six inch snake,
green as mint, soft
as a baby's hand, curled
about my finger
and love it with your love.

With your eyes I see
the crayfish, hard
as a toenail, brown
as the mud beneath
the water's rippled surface
and love it with your love.

With your eyes I see
the nuthatch descend
headfirst the maple trunk,
its blue-gray feathers
light against the bark
and love it with your love.

With your eyes I see
all these and more.
I see the turtle's

painted shell,
the eft's red body
on the crumbling leaves,
the green frog's
leopard spots,
and the snail's bright
trail shining
in the morning sun.

For these I give you thanks,
and for your presence
in their making and unmaking
I give you praise.

Each small life is yours!
In wonder I meet
the richness of your grace
and love you with your love.

IV.

Once more cold is fallen
on the land. Darkness descends early,
and snow wraps the earth in white.
Over the garden
the voice of the dove
is absent.

In desolation we await the birth
of your son.

In the woodlot the opossum,
his naked tail held rigid
an inch above the snow,
ambles unaware.
He knows, if he knows anything,
only your sufficiency,
the completeness of your provision
beneath the wild apple trees.

Across the valley the feet
of the powerful walk over the land
of the weak. They mean wickedness.
They mean to seize
what they will not know.
They mean to speak a word
of emptiness into the fullness
of time. They mean to risk
creation for gain.

In desolation we await the birth
of your son.

Let your broken earth open
to swallow their intentions.
Let the violence of the stone
moving at your command shake
the confidence of their order.

Let your son, this Advent,
be born in power.
Let him come in glory
to claim his own.

Let his word spoken at Creation
echo across the threatened earth,
and let the wicked yield
their feeble claim to dominion
before the rightness of his order.

Then the voice of the dove
descending on us like your spirit
will speak in the garden
and we will answer,
rejoicing in the resurrection
springtime of your Christ,

"Praise you, Father, Son, and Holy Ghost!
Your will be done in us
on earth
as it is in Heaven!"

V.

What once was here, O Lord,
I hold in my imagination's eye—
the forest grown to climax,
the elk, the bear, the wolf
at home, part of your
intention
for this place.

Though I cannot by my labor
change for good the way
this valley yields to willfulness,
one man alone
against devouring man,
I give to you the work
that you have given me.

That the constancy
of my labor might be
my unceasing prayer,

that the fragrance
of humus held to my nose
might rise
an acceptable sacrifice,
that my heart and mind
might incline to no profit
other than your joy,

that my work might be
at last, your work,

bring wholeness to your earth,
the trees I plant
grown to praise the Christ
incarnate in the wood,
the Maker of
elk, and bear, and wolf.